THE POVERTY OF NATIONS

Robert J. Tata

University Press of America,® Inc.
Lanham · Boulder · New York · Toronto · Plymouth, UK

4501 Forbes Boulevard
Suite 200
Lanham, Maryland 20706
UPA Acquisitions Department (301) 459-3366

10 Thornbury Road
Plymouth PL6 7PP
United Kingdom

Printed in the United States of America
British Library Cataloging in Publication Information Available

Library of Congress Control Number: 2012939174
ISBN: 978-0-7618-5942-0 (clothbound : alk. paper)
eISBN: 978-0-7618-5943-7

∞™ The paper used in this publication meets the minimum requirements of American National Standard for Information Sciences—Permanence of Paper for Printed Library Materials, ANSI Z39.48-1992

Table of Contents

List of Tables

Table

Statistical Appendix

Preface

"There are liars, damn liars, and there are statisticians." Originally attributed to Benjamin Disraeli; and popularized by Mark Twain in his "Autobiography." [1]

This book is based on a small mountain of statistics about the world's nations. These statistics describe the physical, economic, social, and political conditions in these nations, status and trends.

Statistics must be used critically. Collection agencies must be trustworthy; inevitable errors must be recognized; attributes assigned to the numbers must be carefully considered; stability in the numbers in time series must exist; and of course, interpretations of the numbers must be realistic and consistent.

The major objective of this book is to reveal which nations fulfill their citizens' needs and which nations do not. Another objective is to find out which nations are making progress in fulfilling human needs, their rate of progress, and which nations are failing to make much progress.

If the analysis succeeds, then we should know why poor nations are poor and what is needed to fulfill the United Nations' "Millennium Development Goals."

Hopefully, more truths than lies will emerge. Only truths can lead to improvement of the human condition worldwide.

Many thanks to Steve Tata, School District of Palm Beach County ESOL Technology Specialist, for his help in formatting this book.

I have relied heavily on the CIA World Factbook, 2011 for information in this book. The CIA collects data from the United Nations, World Bank, individual nation's statistical offices, and their own estimates to publish annually in these books. The books are to inform U.S. State Department and other government agencies so they can do their jobs in relation to the world's nations. Reliability of this information is about the best available.

ENDNOTES

1. Twain, Mark, Autobiography, edited by the Mark Twain project at the Bancroft Library, Berkeley: University of California Press, 2010.

Introduction

Ever since Adam and Eve were expelled from the Garden of Eden, people have had to struggle and innovate to improve their physical and spiritual lives.

The first task to accomplish, obviously, was survival. People harvested nature's bounty to find food, water, oxygen, clothing, shelter, and reproduction. Reproduction is necessary to keep the species going; the others are vital to sustain life. A larger brain capable of storing information and learning from experience and a fully opposable thumb gave people two tools for survival that other animals did not have.

Harnessing fire and sharp tools in hunting, fishing, and gathering activities enhanced the food collection, cooking, defense, and making caves more habitable. Crude painting of animals and everyday scenes on cave walls and ceilings show peoples' desire to express non-material wants. Associations of families and clans to expedite work and defense completed the preconditions for progress from barbarism to civilization.

The first great step towards civilization happened about 10,000 years ago, somewhere in the northern part of the Fertile Crescent. Domestication of plants and animals can truly be called a "REVOLUTION," because they allowed fundamental changes in the way people lived. How did people find out which plants and animals were good to eat and which were not? Trial and error must be the answer, and that must have been traumatic on the survivability of individuals. Change from nomadic to sedentary lives changed many patterns of living, from housing types to division of labor.

Food surpluses from farming and animal husbandry meant that not all people had to be farmers. After farming, the world's oldest profession—not what the popular media would have you believe—probably was soldiering to protect the nascent tribal leaders, merchants, and priests who now inhabited the emerging cities. What you have always heard was the world's oldest profession was added to specialists in home building, artistry, metal working, and a myriad of occupations as people began to acquire specialized skills. Work specialization led to enhanced work productivity and more work specialization. After Egyptian and Sumerian hieroglyphic writing, what probably was the world's first alphabet was developed in Phoenicia, another part of the Fertile Crescent.

The Fertile Crescent is considered "The Cradle of Civilization" for good reason. There has been consistent and progressive improvement in peoples' material and spiritual development in this "Culture Hearth" for more than 10,000 years. The Agricultural Revolution, thanks basically to the irrigation waters and rich alluvial soil of the Tigris and Euphrates Rivers, spawned developments in food productivity, urbanization, religion, writing, artistic and artisan expression, trade, military, and many other aspects of human activity. Barley, wheat, flax, vegetables, cows, pigs, horses, sheep, and goats thrived in this region, giving people abundant stocks of bread, milk, meat, cheese, draft and transportation animals, and leather and wool for the production of fabrics. Abraham, a prophet to Jews, Christians, and Muslims alike, was born about 2,000 BCE near where the Agricultural Revolution started. He is credited with being the world's first monotheist and thus the founder of great religious movements.

One author described this region as a "crossroads" of the world. Overland routes from China, India, inner Asia, Africa, and Europe converged on the Middle East. Sea routes in the Mediterranean and Indian Oceans also had ports of call in Phoenicia, Palestine, the Arabian Peninsula, and the Persian Gulf. Exotic goods, peoples, ideas, and wealth enriched the culture of the region. Cities, city states, and empires evolved from this rich cultural milieu.

Civilizations of Egypt, Persia, Greece, and Rome were the classical forebears of the modern European nation states. After many trials and many errors, the European nation states created the physical and psychological conditions which produced the greatest human well-being the world has ever seen. The Americas, Asia, and Africa have copied these systems with more or less success. No nation has ever achieved a perfect system for guaranteeing high human well-being for all its citizens, if that is even possible. The best we can hope for is that nations will make continuous progress towards that lofty goal.

This book seeks to gauge how well or how poorly the world's nations are doing in their attempts to achieve human well-being.

Chapter One

Human Well-Being: An Analytical System

In the Preamble of the United Nations Charter, the United Nations General Assembly proclaimed the "Universal Declaration of Human Rights." The first sentence of the declaration said that provisions of the document were recognition of:

> "... the inherent dignity and of the equal and inalienable rights of all members of the human family is the foundation of freedom, justice and peace in the world..."[1]

Among the some 30 rights listed, probably the most important are:

1. All humans are born free in dignity and rights.
2. No discrimination can be allowed based on race, color, sex, language, religions, politics, social origin, property, birth or other status.
3. Everyone has the right to life, liberty, and personal security.
4. Everyone is equal before the law.
5. Everyone has the right to privacy.
6. Everyone has a right to live anywhere within their nation.
7. Everyone has the right to own property.
8. Everyone has the right of thought, conscience, and religion.
9. Everyone has the right to freedom of opinion and expression.
10. Everyone has the right to work and receive equal pay for equal work.
11. Everyone has the right to a standard of living for the health and well being of himself and family.
12. Everyone has the right to education.

Forty eight modern nations signed the Universal Declaration of Human Rights in 1948; the eight abstentions were: Belorussia, Czechoslovakia, Poland, Saudi Arabia, Ukraine, South Africa, the USSR, and Yugoslavia. Even though six Muslim nations signed the declaration, on June 30, 2000, the Organization of the Islamic Conference officially recognized the Cairo Declaration on Human Rights in Islam which only recognizes " . . . freedom and right to a dignified life in accordance with the Islamic Shari 'ah."[2] Among other rights restrictions, this document refuses to guarantee religious or gender equality. In a 1993 meeting in Bangkok, Thailand, Asian nations reaffirmed their commitment to the United Nations and the Universal Declaration of Human Rights. Their view is that human rights are universal and interdependent. Also in 1993, the World Conference on Human Rights held in Vienna, Austria, reaffirmed the latter concept, and 150 nations signed their pledge to enforce these rights. In 1998, China adopted the International Covenant on Civil and Political Rights.

In 2000, world leaders at the United Nations adopted eight "Millennium Development Goals" to end extreme poverty in the world by 2015. These eight goals are: 1. Eradicate extreme poverty and hunger, 2. Achieve universal primary education, 3. Promote gender equality and empower women, 4. Reduce child mortality, 5. Improve mental health, 6. Combat HIV/AIDS, malaria and other diseases, 7. Ensure environmental sustainability, and 8. Develop a Global Partnership for Development.

All of these human rights flow from the concepts of "Secular Humanism" which is an outgrowth of European philosophical movements from the 18th and 19th centuries. In turn, Humanism harks back to Socrates whose rationalism demands answers to philosophical questions based on reasoning and the human experience. Europe struggled to fulfill human needs from the end of the Roman Empire, through the creation of modern nation states, through the religious wars of the 16th and 17th centuries, and myriad other international struggles of recent years. Over more than 2000 years, with periods of great progress and periods of agonizing retreat, the concept of human rights to fulfill human needs emerged. While it is clear that Western humanism led the way, the rest of the world and pockets of deprivation in the West seek to extend human well-being to all of humankind. The United Nations is the focal point of this international crusade to promote human well-being by guaranteeing human rights.

Each nation has a set of physical and human resources that can contribute to or detract from human well-being. These resources can be grouped into: Physical System, Social System, Economic System, and Political System. The concept of systems envisions each of these as groups of interacting parts at least partly created by people and organizations to accomplish various goals. All systems should promote human well-being for current and future generations. Because systems evolve over time and are created (influenced) by imperfect humans, they can and do change the dynamic of achieving human well-being. No nation has created perfect human well-being for all its citizens, and given human limitations, perhaps no nation ever can. The best we can hope for is that nations work unceasingly to satisfy human well-being as nations' human and physical systems change over time.

The concept of a nation as a construct composed of 4 interacting systems provides a useful framework for evaluating its strengths and weaknesses in producing human well-being for its citizens. All sources of human well-being can be found in a nation's Physical, Social, Economic, and Political systems. All four interact to enhance or detract from human well-being: soil and climate are used to produce food and income for people; governments tax income to supply people with education and health care; a healthy and educated population supports government and thereby promotes social harmony. And on and on the four systems interact to produce human well-being and a prosperous and progressive nation. Likewise, negative factors and events can cause malfunctions in one or all of a nation's four systems. The latter circumstances cause a decline in human well-being and the many national ill-effects envisioned by the United Nations Universal Declaration of Human Rights.

What are the specific advantages and disadvantages of each of the four systems to add to or subtract from a nation's human well-being? In the next four chapters we will seek answers to this question. In Chapter 6, we will begin our analysis of each of the 151 nations of the world which have more than one million citizens. From this analysis we should be able to determine which nations are satisfying their citizens' human well-being, which nations are not satisfying their citizens' human well-being, and which factors create positive and which factors create negative effects. By making comparisons of conditions in 1960 and comparing them to conditions in 2010, we will be able to judge whether a nation has achieved the United Nations' Millennium Goals, is making progress towards achieving these goals, or continues to suffer a lack of human well-being. The causes of the differences between national development—underdevelopment among nations should also be made clear.

ENDNOTES

1. United Nations, *Charter of the United Nations*, San Francisco: United Nations Conference on International Organization, 1945.

2. See: Littman, David, "Universal Human Rights, and 'Human Rights in Islam'," Midstream, New York, February/March 1999.

Chapter Two
The Physical System

What are specific contributions to human well-being that each system can and should provide? Some of the most basic human needs come from the Physical System, also called the physical environment. All humans need oxygen, water, warmth, and food to survive—these are basic needs supplied or limited by the physical resource base. Yet nature can give more benefits. Size, shape, global location, and material resources are nature given; people and technology can enhance physical resources, or in some cases, diminish the existing useful resources. For instance, trees were somewhat of a nuisance to American colonial farmers in New England. Granted lumber, nuts, fruits, maple syrup, tannin, and pitch were useful products, but farmers wanted land cleared to plant their crops. Much of the prime forests were cut down and taken out of the reserve of renewable resources. Two examples might help to illustrate how Mother Nature gives and takes away.

France

Size and Shape

France is a good example of the bounty of nature. With more than 246,167 square miles, France is slightly smaller than Texas, and it does not have any extensive areas of wasteland. The population density is only 259 people per square mile, which ranks the country just a little more than average to all the world's nations. The shape of France is roughly circular which implies easy access and low transportation costs from the center of the nation to its international borders. Lack of extreme differences in surface elevations strengthens this observation. In terms of the value of agriculture, forestry, and fishing (not including minerals) production per capita, France ranks 9th in the world. This is another indicator of nature's bounty.

Absolute Location

Located in the higher middle latitudes (42°-52° north), France benefits from its northwestern European location with long coastlines on the North Atlantic Ocean and Mediterranean Sea. Most of the country enjoys a Marine West Coast climate with long growing season, adequate rainfall, and moderate winters. The southern region has a Mediterranean climate with long and hot dry summers and mild rainy winters. Forrests and soils contribute excellent agriculture and forest products. France is the world leader in fine wine production, a high value added primary industry. Grains, fruits, vegetables, and livestock all make a major economic boost to a productive economy. Fisheries in the North Atlantic and Mediterranean also add to varied and diverse food base. French cuisine is world renown and it is based on fresh ingredients.

Relative Location

Location in the northwestern section of the rich European Continent is another major physical advantage. The negative past of innumerable wars among strong neighbors has evolved into strong positive international relations economically and politically. Belgium, Germany, Switzerland, Italy, Spain, and even England through the Chunnel have land borders with France and these generate more than half of its trade business. While the French would probably never admit it, the cultural stimulation from highly developed neighbors has greatly benefited the development of French culture. Mountains, forests, beaches, navigable rivers, and picturesque plains are physical amenities that satisfy most environmental tastes. Most of the country is in the Marine West Coast climate, which means there are the traditional seasons of summer, fall, winter, and spring, whose transformations many people believe are stimulating; a little something for all outdoors enthusiasts. France is one of the world's greatest tourist destinations.

Resources

Soils, forests, fisheries, fuels, and minerals all contribute to France's wealth. Wheat, cereals, wine grapes, potatoes, sugar beets, cattle, sheep, goats, pigs, and chickens are produced in large quantities. Oak and olive trees, pines, and hardwoods feed industries from furniture to wine barrels. Both Atlantic and Mediterranean waters yield large fish catches. Minerals produced include coal, iron ore, bauxite, uranium, oil, and natural gas.

Virtually all aspects of France's physical environment contribute to the nation's varied sources of wealth and human well-being. Not many nations in the world enjoy this bounty from nature.

MONGOLIA

Mongolia's physical environment places severe handicaps on the nation's attempts at modernization. This nation ranks 101 on our scale of the productivity of its physical environment. (See: Table Ap.1, Agriculture Value Added Per Capita in the Statistical Appendix). This is a "Below Average" ranking among the world's nations. This ranking is probably too high because of the nation's sparse population and the fact that agriculture, which includes herding, comprises about one-third of the overall economy.

The country is more than twice the size of Texas, yet it has only about 3 million people; there are more horses than people in Mongolia. Indeed, these small tough horses provided the mobility to create the "Golden Horde" empire of Ghengis Kahn. Mongolia's population density is one of the worlds lowest. About half the population lives near the capital city of Ulan Bator, in the north central part of the country; large sections of the west and south are virtually unpopulated. The nation has a long, oval shape and stretches from 85 ° to 120 ° east longitude. And from 48° to 54° north latitude, its location has the depressing sobriquet of "the dead inner heart of Asia."

Only three other nations border this inland nation, and these comprise the sparsely populated portions of Siberia, north China, and eastern Kazakhstan. Isolation is a key national characteristic. There is no ocean coastline, no major lakes, and no navigable rivers; lack of water transportation raises transportation costs. Located in the higher middle latitudes and far from large bodies of water that moderate temperature extremes, Mongolia has a cold and dry climate. The Gobi Desert in the south blends into the arid cold grasslands in the north. Many people are forced to lead a nomadic life.

Contact with the rest of the world is tenuous and difficult, even in this era of fast jet planes. Historians tell us that Mongolia reached the zenith of its power as a nation in the 13th century with Ghengis Kahn. The benefits of close contact, social, economic, and political interactions among neighbors, eludes Mongolia even to this day. Pessimists might conclude that isolation from the world's chaotic modern events is a benefit, but that is a contrarian view and it contradicts the modern concept of globalization.

Mongolia's climate is cold desert in the southern section of the country, the remainder being a cold steppe. Almost all of the territory gets less than 10 inches of rain, which under cool annual temperatures supports only short grass vegetation. There is a short and hot summer, and a long very cold winter. Nomadic herding of goats, sheep, cattle, and horses is the major land use; such extensive use of the land never supports many people. The unique breed of Mongolian horses are small, tough, and have great endurance. Carrying Ghengis Kahn to a world empire, this heritage has carried over so that modern Mongolian children are expert riders. High mountains cover the western half of the country and this rough terrain further degrades the contribution of the physical environment for useful purposes. The rest of the nation is composed of dissected plateaus and mountains which average between 2,000 and 5,000 foot elevations.

Vegetation and soils reflect the dry and cold climate. Steppe short grass and desert scrub covers most of Mongolia and these provide poor pasturage; that is the reason why nomadic herding is a major part of agriculture. Soils tend to be alkaline and crops only find favorable conditions in alluvial exotic river valleys. Droughts, floods, hail, strong winds, and frigid winters add to the poor productivity of the physical environment.

Minerals provide the country with some export earnings. Copper, coal, tin, tungsten, molybdenum, gold, phosphates, nickel, and zinc support an active mining industry. Energy production depends on fossil fuels, principally coal and oil, part of which must be imported.

Overall, the physical environment detracts from creating human well-being in Mongolia. Even its large size makes communications within the country and externally to other countries expensive and difficult. Rough terrain, harsh climate, alkaline soils, limited mineral resources, and remote location with regard to the world's major population centers all contribute to Mongolia's poverty.

The indicator to evaluate the contributions of the Physical System to a nation's human well-being is the amount of value added from agriculture, forestry, and fishing to the national economy. Granted that people can build infrastructure that enhances the productivity of the physical environment, natural conditions must be favorable for production to occur. Nations with rich economies sometimes concentrate investment on manufacturing and service industries, thereby deemphasizing agriculture and other primary businesses. Witness the 'soil bank' and conservation programs in the United States over the past half century. Agricultural land was actually taken out of production during these programs. Developed nations generally have about 2% of their GDP come from agriculture, while poor countries' agricultural sectors contribute as much as 85% of their GDPs. With all these caveats, the amount of value added of agricultural output is a reasonably good indicator of the productivity of the Physical Systems of nations.

The 2010 data gives us the status of the Physical System's productivity; more importantly, the change in productivity from 1960 to 2010 describes the trend in productivity over the past 50 years.

Chapter Three
The Social System

A social system describes the people and the interactions among people within a nation, and it is a basic factor in promoting or limiting human well-being. A social system should promote the growth of individuals in such characteristics as social cohesion, growth of humanness, positive social mores, and cooperation among people. We need to know the total population, population density, growth rates, age distributions, ethnic divisions, educational and skills status, rural-urban characteristics, social stratification, and any other defining traits. Age distribution is a critical indicator. Poor nations tend to have more of their populations under 15 years old. Children are considered to be consumers rather than producers and they create burdens on the rest of the population to support them. Those over 65 years old can be similarly considered.

Next we need to know about social dynamics and organization. Is there cohesiveness in society or crippling divisiveness? A key element is the educational system. Are there opportunities for people to be "all they can be," or are there barriers to personal growth and improved lifestyles? Based on their historical experiences, do people benefit from positive or suffer from negative mores developed over time? Is the society open to change? What kinds of dialogues exist to effect positive change and what punishments exist for retrogressive behavior? Does religion, peer pressure, or other forces influence behavior?

Abraham Maslow's "Hierarchy of Human Needs" is a useful paradigm for evaluating societies' contribution to human well-being.[1] He postulated human needs in the form of a pyramid. The basic needs—food, water, oxygen, health, body temperature—are obvious needs to keep the body alive. If a person lacks any of these needs, he/she will exert every effort to attain them and will be fixated on these efforts. Once these needs are satisfied, safety and security needs become paramount. Lack of this need creates tension and coping behavior that detracts from initiative and productive activity. If safety and security needs are met, people begin to think about "love and belonging." While procreation is at the lowest level, to replace deceased people, this need emphasizes the feelings about belonging to groups which share goals and psychological well-being. The family is the basic group at this level of human needs. Deprivation of this need leads to alienation from society and anti-social behavior. The next need is self-esteem. People need to feel that they have mastered some aspect of life, either in a profession, leadership role, captain of industry, charitable works, skill, or intellectual endeavor. The more ladders to self-esteem that exist in a society, the better off the individual and the whole society will be. At the top of human achievement is what Maslow called "self-actualization." Such people have gained a high level of self-esteem, and beyond this, further enhance society by giving back various forms of voluntary goods and services in their own country, or perhaps in the world-wide community.

Are these concepts limited to western society, or do they have universal applicability?

> As I traveled across the globe for nearly six decades, I have found that people exhibit remarkable similarities that by no stretch of the imagination can be construed as resulting from culture, history, language, or chance. All people appear motivated by an inbred striving for self-esteem that is in large part fostered by the approval of others.[2]

While specific aspects of self-esteem might vary in form from a chess champion in Russia to a master hunter in a less developed society, the fact that human needs exist is universal. Even something as basic as facial expressions have been shown to be correctly interpreted by widely varied cultures.[3] Thus we can conclude that healthy societies provide the mechanisms and the freedoms for people to move upward in Maslow's hierarchy of human needs. Unfulfilled needs can lead to social disaffection, and in worse cases, suicide, or open rebellion.

Japan. Of the world's major nations, Japan ranks first with the lowest infant mortality rates with only 2.79 deaths per 1,000 live births. Tiny Sweden ranks slightly higher with a ranking of only 2.75 infant deaths. The world average is 30.2 for 224 of the world's political units, including the smallest of islands. In 1960, Japan ranked 16th in the world among 151 nations; a nice rise in human well-being from 1960 to 2010.

Japan's population of 127,540,000 ranks the country 10th in the world in total population. With an area of a little more than half that of Texas, Japan's population density is 13th in the world. High population density can be a great concern, especially when the resource base is limited, and the population growth rate is high. Malthus pointed to this dilemma in the 18th century. In 1930, Japan suffered from exactly this problem, and this condition was a major factor in that nation's Imperialist ambitions. Technology has solved both problems. Population growth is now negative -.139, the 13th lowest growth rate in the world. The Japanese legislature recently discussed the population problem of depopulation. While space and natural resources are still limited, urbanization and high technology manufacturing and services have made Japan one of the world's wealthiest societies.

Japan's society was thoroughly feudal and isolationist in 1868 when changes began to occur. Contact with Europeans and Americans demonstrated how backward the society was, and the Japanese rebelled to change this situation. Privileged classes and regionalism were replaced by a strong central government by 1898, and the country started technological, military, and industrial revolutions. Successful wars with China in 1894-95 and Russia in 1904-05 signaled the emergence of Japan as an international power. Economic advancement and urbanization brought many societal changes. However, obedience to the wishes of the Emperor, considered a god-king up to 1945 and the old fashioned feudal mores limited the personal freedoms in Japan that the western societies enjoyed.

The unconditional surrender in 1945 and occupation by U.S. forces transformed Japanese society. One can only wonder what Japan would be like today if Russia was the occupying force after WWII. The United States demanded that the Emperor renounce his claim to be a god and implemented a new constitution modeled after its own. One other major contribution to modernization, carrying over to the present time, was for the United States to assume the bulk of defense costs. Japan was thus able to mobilize all domestic resources and devote them to modernization. What Japan failed to achieve in war—an international equality with the west in economic, social, and political attainment—it achieved as a defeated nation in peace-time.

Today Japan has a homogeneous, well-educated, mature, hard-working, obedient, peaceful, prosperous, and progressive society. As one simple example, consider the fact that the largely isolationist society in the first half of the twentieth century did not produce one Nobel laureate. Since 1949, there have been 16 Japanese Nobel laureates, mostly in physics and chemistry; most of these scholars were trained in Japanese universities. Five had training in the United States. Young Japanese traveling abroad look, behave, and even have the body language of the best elements of American young people. To continue the chauvinism ad nauseam, the Japanese even play baseball on a par with the best players in the U.S.

Every statistic about Japan's population indicates a modern and privileged society. Two thirds are in the productive age cohort of 15-65 years; life expectancy is 79 for males and 86 for females; literacy is 99%; ethnicity is 99% Japanese—Japan rejects the idea that ethnic diversity is a desirable population trait; 84% practice Shinto or Buddhism; 66% is urban; GDP/capita in Purchasing Power Parity is $34,200, one of the world's highest; and unemployment is negligible. Educational and institutional opportunities are abundant for improving the individual's status in society. The status of women in Japan has improved in recent years, but gender discrimination is greater than in most western nations. Social mores are Westernized and modern, although the nation strives to maintain traditional values and social institutions.[4]

Ethiopia. Ethiopia has one of the world's highest infant mortality rates with 81 infant deaths per 1,000 live births. This is almost 3 times the world average. Add to this the fact that the average life expectancy at birth is 55 years, 12 years lower than the world average, and the picture of a society in deep trouble emerges. Some 80 million people in a country about twice the size of Texas, makes for a moderate population density. Rugged terrain over most of the country and drought in the east make the 3.2% population growth rate problematical. Periodic drought conditions create food shortages and great human suffering.

Ethiopia may be the original home where humans developed. Lucy, the skeletal remains of a hominid, was found here, and she may have roamed the area 2.3 million years ago. Other hominid remains date from 6 million years ago. The nation is one of the most ancient organized political entities, dating back to ancient Egyptian and Greek civilizations. Orthodox Christians, Coptic Christians, Muslims, and Jews all contributed to the historical cultural melange. Even though many people remained isolated in high mountain clusters, the eastern and northern valleys and lowlands saw the mixing of many nomadic tribes.

Today the Ethiopian population is heterogeneous in the extreme. There are some 80 ethnic groups and 84 indigenous languages; literacy is less than 36%. There are more than 200,000 refugees from Somalia and these people are from the lowest socio-economic classes. About 80% of the labor force earns a meager living from the soil and still food must be imported. Some experts claim that with proper modern farming, Ethiopia not only could feed itself, but could supply all of Europe's food imports as well. A big agricultural program in the 1980s relocated about 2 million farmers into the potentially rich agricultural zone in the west, but malaria and serious infrastructure problems sabotaged the plan. The country is still unable to feed itself.

Except for a short interlude of Italian domination between 1936 to 1941, Ethiopia did not suffer the effects of European Colonialism.

Abyssinia was known as an organized kingdom to the ancient Egyptians, Greeks, and Romans. Comprising the territories of modern Ethiopia and Eritrea, the Abyssinians had developed lucrative sea borne trade with India and China. The people were a mixture of Hamitic tribes from southwest Asia and Semitic tribes from the Arabian Penninsula. King Menelik I, the legendary Jewish ruler in 950 B.C., is believed to have been the son of Solomon and Sheba. Menelik is believed to have been the start of a ruling dynasty that lasted for 2,900 years and only ended with the overthrow of Emperor Haille Selassie in 1974. Ethiopia had extensive trade with Egypt, Greece, and Rome, enriching the society in financial and cultural terms. Military power spread the nation's influence in all directions. Coptic Christians migrated into Ethiopia in the 4th Century AD and their influence has remained into the modern era; 61% of the population professes Christianity today. The height of the country's influence and foreign contacts peaked in the 5th century of modern times. Maurading Muslim armies pushed Ethiopians back into the more easily defended mountainous interior, but this retreat isolated the nation from its international contacts, making the society reclusive and stagnant.

Political turbulence also contributed to social and economic decline. While Ethiopia escaped the evils of Islamic and European Colonialism, ancient feudal wars and modern wars among neighbors and periodic natural disasters weakened the economic and social systems. Whereas neighboring states modernized, Ethiopia remained feudal under its almost unbroken chain of absolute rulers. Rural settlement patterns, predominance of agricultural workers, and the diversity of many tribes have retarded the modernization of social institutions that are needed to promote the attainment of higher human needs. A Communist coup in

1991 after extreme political chaos for years, a war with Somalia in 1988, and a border war with Eritrea in 1995 made a bad situation worse. Russian advisors, 15,000 Cuban troops, Somalia and Eritrean refugees, and dislocated local tribes completed the political, social, and economic dysfunction. If that were not enough, terrible droughts over the past 30 years disrupted any progress in development; the result was a perpetration and institutionalization of social backwardness. It is no wonder that Ethiopia has serious social problems compared to the rest of the world's nations.

Infant Mortality Rates for 2010 will give us an idea about how well each nation's Social System is satisfying its citizens' human well-being. Changes in Infant mortality from 1960 to 2010 indicate progress each nation has made in its Social System to promote human well-being. Failure to experience progress in the Social System will indicate serious societal dysfunctions.

Many factors cause infant mortality rates to be high or low around the globe. One strong factor is environmental health; contaminated water, for example, causes many deaths of babies in poor countries; endemic and epidemic diseases also cause many deaths. The educational levels of parents, pre-natal and post-natal care, existence and affordability of medical care, nutrition, and internal or international violence also raise or lower infant mortality rates. It is plain from these examples that infant mortality rates are affected by physical, psychological, and institutional factors. Nations with low infant mortality rates are the most favored in social human well-being in all its facets, and those with highest rates are those that have low social human well-being. Infant Mortality rates will be a good indicator of the status and trends in nations social human well-being.

ENDNOTES

1. See: Maslow, Abraham, *Motivation And Personality*, New York: Harper and Row, 1954.

2. Greenspan, Alan, The *Age Of Turbulence: An Adventure In A New World*, New York: The Penguin Press, 2007.

3. Gladwell, Malcom, *Blink: The Power Of Thinking Without Thinking*, New York: Little Brown and Company, 2004, p. 199.

4. See: Seward, Jack, *The Japanese*, New York: William Morrow and Company, 1972.

Chapter Four
The Economic System

"Money makes the world go round, the world go round, the world go round . . ." At least these are the lyrics of a tune from "Caberet." From Economics 101, we should probably modify those sentiments to: "Useful goods and services make the world go round, etc." As economists like to say, wealth is a necessary but not a sufficient condition for human well-being. Wealth buys hospitals, schools, trained professionals, leisure time, modern infrastructure, good housing, myriad markets, entrepreneurs, international contacts, and modernization potential. Gross Domestic Product Per Capita (GDP/Capita), defined as all the goods and services at market value produced in a nation in one year, divided by the nation's population, is the most common single statistic used to measure the development status of any nation. GDP underestimates the productivity of the poorest nations because work such as building a house, growing food, making clothing, and providing transportation are done within the family; thus these goods and services never get into marketplace accounting. One attempt to remedy this statistical disparity is to transform GDP into "Purchasing Power Parity" (PPP), which standardizes a "basket of goods" so that living costs among various nations are comparable. PPP is also standardized over time so that the effects of variable currency values over time are taken into consideration. PPP values will be used in all statistical series in this book to make comparisons of nations' economic productivity over time and space more valid.

Adam Smith's 1776 book, The Wealth of Nations, was a bible for Laissez Faire economics and the power of "The Market" for driving a nation's economy.[1] Land, Labor, and Capital were considered the factors that drive economic activity, and individuals pursuing their self interest in acquiring wealth was the natural path toward societal economic well-being. Land is defined as the total physical resource base; labor includes not only the physical activity of producing goods and services, but also the skills and inventive capacity (entrepreneurship) of people; capital includes the technological processes to convert resources and component parts into goods and services, and the infrastructure needed to make and distribute goods and services. Agriculture and incipient manufacturing were the major economic activities in 1776, described as "primary and secondary" industries. Today, services or tertiary industries are the driving force of highly productive economies.

Primary industries are all those in which nature plays a vital role in the production process. Agriculture, forestry, fishing, hunting, and mining are the major subdivisions. Our measure of the productivity of the natural environment—Agricultural Value Added—takes the share of GDP from these economic sectors, less mining. Exclusion of mining means that nations with large oil deposits do not distort the comparisons of the wealth derived from the physical environment. Non-renewable resources such as coal, iron ore, oil, even gold and silver are "temporary wealth." After they are dug out of the ground, all you have left are big holes in the ground. Renewable resources such as fertile soil, fisheries, and valuable forests can contribute to national wealth indefinitely if they are properly managed.

The industrial revolution, starting about 1760 in England to about 1960 as it spread to Belgium, France, Germany, the U.S., and Japan brought previously unheard of wealth to those nations. Secondary industry (manufacturing) harnessed inanimate energy to transform raw materials and component parts into useful products of virtually unlimited varieties, constrained almost exclusively by entrepreneurs' fertile inventiveness and innovation of new useful products to make life easier and more enjoyable.

Manufacture of textiles and various household goods started the Industrial Revolution, and technological innovation in machinery, power sources, and new products brought manufacturing to its zenith towards the end of the twentieth century. Today, many of the low value-added goods such as textiles and household items are produced in poor countries that have low labor costs, while highly complex manufacture of technologically advanced goods such as medical equipment and communications equipment remain in the rich countries.

The manufacture of automobiles used to be a major measure of the productivity of a nation's entire economy. Automobiles need large numbers of complicated sub-parts so that automobile manufacture spawned the advent of many industries such as engines, mini-computers, automotive electronics, transmission systems, brake systems, tires, sheet metal, glass and plastics, and many others. Even within the automotive industry, research and development and design of new models employ many technical experts and absorb a lot of capital inputs. The space industry has spawned a revolution in tele-communications, computer applications, miniaturization of complex systems, fuels, engines, the internet, and new construction materials. Innovations in these and related industries boost the productivity of tertiary industries.

Tertiary covers all occupations in which human skills play an important role in the production process, from selling lottery tickets on a street corner to developing nuclear physics for new power sources. Science, usually developed in universities and research institutes, creates new technologies, while business administration innovates goods and services that fulfill human wants. Unfortunately, the low productivity tertiary industries such as household and other servants, sales persons, personal grooming, sanitation workers, gardeners, fruit and vegetable harvesters, and general laborers do not require highly trained skills, do not produce high value added-goods and services, and therefore, they do not command high salaries. Highly trained tertiary operators produce high value-added goods and services and their work places are in nations whose primary and secondary industries are also highly productive.

Globalization is a modern economic concept which involves internationalization of the factors of production, and the final output and its marketing of goods and services. Capital, technology, and transportation / communications are now easily mobile around the world so that many nations may participate in manufacturing. Cheap labor is still a major draw to attract simple manufacturing processes. Japan's industrialization was started by the production of cheap textiles, ceramic and glass products, wood trinkets and housewares, tools, and toys. "Made in Japan" on an item in the 1950s and 60s almost always meant low prices and goods that would break and be discarded within a year of purchase. Now the Japanese are known as the best producers of automobiles, machinery, audio-video equipment, and technical instruments. Other nations such as China, India, and Brazil are trying to duplicate the Japanese model of economic growth. Globalization of manufacturing and services has raised incomes in many parts of the world.

United States. With only 4% of the world's population, the United States produces about 25% of all the GDP in the world. It takes the combined economies of all 27 of the rich European Union nations to equal this economic output. Japan and China each produce about 9% of the world's GDP, while Germany contributes 6%, and France produces about 5%. The five largest economies produce some 54% of the world's GDP. China's rise to one of the world's largest economies is a recent phenomenon, and this spectacular growth has been caused mostly by globalization. The other four, United States, Japan, Germany, and France might be considered to have "mature economies," because their economic growth has occurred over more than 100 years, and they have an average of 76% of their labor forces in highly productive tertiary industries. China's tertiary comprises only 33% of its labor force, and much of this is in low productivity services.

As this is being written in the middle of the worst world-wide recession since the 1930s, it seems incongruous to hold up the United States as the paragon of world economies. Yet, "business cycles" are widely recognized as "normal" occurrences in a capitalist economy. History shows that the United States has suffered many economic downturns in the past 150 years, but the productive forces are always strong enough and the internal markets are strong enough to empower another period of growth. The U.S. economy is maturing, a scenario in which low paying manufacturing jobs and even low cost tertiary jobs are being outsourced overseas; in this stage of economic development new jobs need higher and higher technical inputs and innovation of high technology products are paramount.

The example of the historical growth of the U.S. economy will provide insights on the stages of economic development. A pre-industrial economy is one in which farming, fishing, forestry, and simple handicrafts employ most people. Farming in the New England Colonies was not a productive enterprise. Forests provided the raw materials for building fishing and trading ships, and New Englanders quickly took to the seas. Manufacturing, literally "making things by hand" from the Latin root words, was done to make tools, horseshoes, harnesses, nails, hinges, and other iron objects, made by hand by the village blacksmiths. Town names such as Valley Forge, Old Forge (many of these), Pigeon Forge, Clifton Forge, Providence Forge, and Warrior Forge all indicated the site of blacksmith shops. Low grade bog iron and charcoal from the forests supplied the indispensable raw materials.

Entrepreneurship—people who anticipated markets and gathered workers, capital, energy, and productive capacity to fulfill a perceived need—spurred the growth of manufacturing. In the small central Connecticut town of New Britain, later to become the "Hardware City of the World" in the 1920s to the 1950s, an entrepreneur made pots and pans out of tin. Tin cooking gear was lighter and easier to clean than ironware, and women wanted them to make cooking a less burdensome chore. The Yankee Peddlar loaded these and many other household items on wagons, preparing for sales trips to the far flung rural markets in the Spring and Summer months. Connecticut got its nickname "The Nutmeg State" because it was said that Yankee Peddlars were such shrewd traders that they could sell the housewives wooden nutmegs.

Industrial espionage gave a boost to American industrialization. Samuel Slater was apprenticed to a partner of Richard Arkwright in 1782 in England. He worked in a factory which was equipped with the new spinning and carding machines for making textiles. The machines and those who worked on them were forbidden by law to leave England. Slater disguised himself, in the best James Bond tradition, and emigrated to the United States in 1789. Having memorized the machinery, Slater took a job in Pawtucket, Rhode Island, got financing from a local capitalist, and he set up the new machines in 1793. Success in this enterprise allowed Slater to create 13 different partnerships, and new textile mills were founded in Rhode Island, Connecticut, Massachusetts, and New Hampshire. Samuel Slater thereby earned the title as the "Father of U.S. Manufacturing."

New Britain, Connecticut represents the benefits from an early start and the resulting disaster when advantages from manufacturing move elsewhere.[2] In 1843, Frederick Stanley founded Stanley Bolt Manufactory to produce wrought iron door bolts and other iron hardware. Fourteen years later, his cousin, Henry Stanley founded Stanley Rule and Level which made the best carpenters' plane in the world. 1920 saw the merging of the cousins' companies into The Stanley Works, today a world-wide firm which makes some of the world's best tools and hardware. In the 100 years after 1811, nine major firms were founded by local entrepreneurs to manufacture tools, household appliances, hardware, and ball bearings. More U.S. patents were held by New Britain residents than the residents of any other U.S. city. More than 80% of all jobs were created by these nine firms, and the city grew from 3,009 in 1850 to 83,411 in 1970.

In 1965, General Electric raided Landers, Frary, and Clark just to get control of that company's electric coffee percolator, then the world's best. The rest of the company was quickly run into the ground. The company went out of business, and New Britain's manufacturing operations began their nearly complete decline. Other firms were bought out by national firms, or relocated to more favorable locations. The only major factory left in New Britain is The Stanley Works. Even this firm threatened to move its home office to Bermuda, but the federal government prevented this "Globalization" and loss of jobs and corporate taxes. The town is now a "service center," several major highways having been built to cross in New Britain, and its teachers College has been elevated to university status. Another new unsavory function of the once proud "Hardware City of the World" is to house immigrants and drug dealers in several run down former worker neighborhoods.

Entrepreneurship is the dynamic factor that drives an economy to increased productivity. Entrepreneurship of course includes new and useful products, but it also comprises the application of "start-up-capital" to open up new markets. Elements of the social, economic, and political environments all contribute to the encouragement of entrepreneurship. Education, especially having a good system of research institutes is vital. Shunpei Yamazaki of Semi Conductor Energy Laboratory in Atsugi, Japan, holds 1,811 U.S. patents, more than three times the number held by Thomas A. Edison. The economic system of a nation must hold out economic rewards and social rewards for entrepreneurship, offering wealth and prestige to inventors. The political system must provide laws that protect intellectual property from competitors, just as companies guard their patented products from pirating by competitors. Capitalist firms want rewards for their entrepreneurial activities and the ability to make profits to justify their capital expenditures.

Yet all this may not be enough. Malcom Gladwell's book, "Outliers: the Story of Success," describes how talented people, from The Beatles to Bill Gates, must have the initial talent and drive to succeed, then they must expend 10,000 hours in pursuing their specialties to achieve successful outcomes.[3] Competition among producers is another force for innovation. A team of engineers from IBM in the mid 1970s "invented" the personal computer, their efforts being pushed by Steve Jobs of Apple, Hewlett Packard, Texas Instruments, Dell, and others to capture markets with improved products. Information technology has transformed the economic and social environments of all the world's nations. Some even believe the spread of information to virtually everyone in several societies helped to defeat some totalitarian regimes.

Unquestionably, innovative technology keeps modern economies productive. Technological development cannot be predicted, perhaps not even programmed as part of an economic system. The best any nation can do is to keep the conditions for entrepreneurship viable to allow creative people to innovate and drive economies forward. Science creates new technology, and business administration adopts the new technology to new uses. The U.S. space program required many innovations which eventually got transferred into new consumer goods from telecommunications, to electronic positioning devices to new construction materials to new food products. Unpredictable, but vital in promoting economic growth, entrepreneurship is facilitated by the U.S. economic, social, and political systems.

As the U.S. population expanded and moved westward after 1803, outstanding natural resources for agriculture and industry awaited the pioneers. A railroad boom from 1830 to 1860 facilitated the movement of people and bulky goods. A canal system boosted barge traffic as well. In 1869 the first transcontinental railroad was completed; in 1916 the rail network reached its greatest extent and road extension began its growth. Iron ore, and coal gave rise to iron and steel production, which in turn supplied the materials for railroads and various vehicles and engines. Excellent crop and grazing land led to a very productive food industry. Many of these endeavors were financed by capital from Europe, especially England. Entrepreneurs such as Eli Whitney, Thomas Colt, Robert Fulton, Thomas Edison, the Wright Brothers, Henry Ford, Cyrus McCormick, John Deere, Elias Howe, Dr. H. Edwards (personal computer), Bill Gates, Steve Jobs and others were innovators who helped build the nation's productive capacity over 200 years of growth. The United States economy became the World's preeminent economy and a larger part of the total population attained middle class status than that of any other major nation in history.

Other nations in the modern era are following the U.S. model of free enterprise economic development to economic prosperity, including former command economies of Russia, China, and nations of Eastern Europe. Globalization and technology transfer have accelerated this process. Capitalism in all its variants has proved to be the best engine for economic development for most countries. In 1960, South Korea with a PPP/capita of $1,513, ranked 104th in the world; North Korea with a PPP/capita of $1,597, ranked 98th in the world. In 2010, South Korea had a PPP/capita of $23,825, ranking that nation 27th in the world; while North Korea with a PPP/capita of $1,582 ranked 119th in the world. In 50 years, North Korea has actually declined in economic well-being, one of the few nations in the world to have retrogressed during this period of spectacular rise in world economic development.

Just as Samuel Slater "borrowed" England's technology in textile machinery to start the U.S. economy's growth, technology transfer today aids many nations' economic growth. Speaking of the phenomenal growth in information generation, artificial thinking, data management, and decision making that characterizes the advanced nations, Jamais Cascio says:

> "The bad news is that these divergent paths may exacerbate cultural divides created by already divergent languages and beliefs. National rivalries often emphasize cultural differences, but for now we're still standard human beings. What happens when different groups quite literally think in very, very different ways?
>
> The good news though, is that this diversity of thought can also be a strength. Coping with the various world-historical dangers we face will require the greatest possible insight, creativity, and innovation. Our ability to build the future we want—not just a future we can survive—depends on our capacity to understand complex relationships of the world's systems, to take advantage of

> the diversity of knowledge and experiences our civilization embodies, and to fully appreciate the implications of our choices. Such an ability is increasingly within our grasp. The noocene awaits."[4]

Obviously, the technologically advanced nations will rocket ahead of the poor nations in economic development. The important question is how the favored nations can assist the poor nations to forge ahead. Cell phone technology was an outgrowth of the space industry, dominated by the U.S. and Russia. Now poor nations do not need to build expensive infrastructure to improve their information flow. They can merely "borrow" the new technology from world suppliers.

Haiti. Haiti has actually declined in the production of goods and services per capita in the years from 1960 to 2010. Two-thirds of Haiti's income is still produced from agriculture, and the agricultural sector is hopelessly backward. Overpopulation, poor agricultural resources, and primitive technology dooms the country to poor agricultural production. Farms average less than 5 acres, many of the farms are on steep slopes, soils are poor and overused, and climate is arid in some places and subject to severe tropical storms in others. Fishing is virtually a subsistence activity; animal husbandry is almost non-existant; and forests have long ago been denuded by cutting for charcoal, the predominant cooking fuel. Manufacturing is often of the handicraft variety, producing clothing, stitching baseballs, and basic preparation of food products. Service industries are from the low technology types, and lack of capital and technology has caused long-term stagnation. Haiti's economy displays the classical dysfunctions of the vicious circle of poverty. International aid has had almost no impact on inducing economic growth. Haiti's GDP (PPP) in 1960 was $1,781 and it was $1,198 in 2010.

Haiti is proud of the fact that after the United States, Haiti was the first nation in the Western Hemisphere to gain its independence in 1804. As a slave-plantation economy for almost three centuries under the French, wealth was produced in sugar, cotton, indigo, and coffee. Adam Smith called Haiti the wealthiest and most important sugar producer in the Caribbean. After independence was won in a bloody revolution, the plantation system was destroyed and it was replaced by a peasant based agriculture of small farms. Most of the Caucasian upper classes and even some of the mulatto upper classes were killed or driven into exile. Unfortunately, this led to the demise of the entrepreneurial/capitalist class and the experienced administrators. There is an apocryphal story that after the bitter struggle for independence, the victorious former slaves ripped the white center of the French tricolor and stitched the red part to the blue to make the new nation's flag.

Stripped of its economic, social, and political leaders, Haiti's economy and human well-being deteriorated. A high population growth rate, limited agricultural resources, and lack of capital and entrepreneurs for encouraging new industries helped to create disorder in society and a steady decline in the human con dition. Today, Haiti is the prototype of an overpopulated nation with poor prospects for the future.[5]

Haiti's neighbor on the island of Hispaniola, the Dominican Republic, shared much of Haiti's history up until 1964-66 when the United States stopped a left-wing coup and started massive aid to rebuild the nation's economy. Political stability came first, then economic growth followed. Both countries had almost equal GDP/Capita (PPP) of less than $2,000 in 1960; by 2010, Haiti's had slipped to $1,198 from $1,781, while the Dominican Republic's figures rose from $1,553 to $8,600. Both are small and relatively poor Caribbean nations, but at least the Dominican Republic has experienced substantial progress in economic human well-being while Haiti has not.

GDP/Capita (In this book expressed in Purchasing Power Parity) is the world-wide standard for measuring the productivity of a nation's economy. The PPP number gives us a stable indicator in time and in space to compare nations' performances. Thus we have a reliable indicator for comparing nations' economic status in 2010 and the progress they have made in the past half century.

Endnotes

1. See: Smith, Adam, *An Inquiry Into The Nature And Causes Of The Wealth Of Nations*, New York: Random House, The Modern Library, 1994.

2. See: Tata, Robert J., "Problems Of Industrial Old Age: New Britain, Ct, A Case Study," MA Thesis, Syracuse University, 1961.

3. See: Gladwell, Malcom, *Blink: The Power Of Thinking Without Thinking*, New York: Little Brown and Company, 2004.

4. Cascio, Jamais, "Get Smart," The Atlantic, Vol 304, no 1, July-August 2009, pp. 94-100.

5. See: Tata, Robert J., *Haiti: Land Of Poverty*, Washington, DC: University Press of America, 1982.

Chapter Five
The Political System

A nation's political system must choose leaders, provide national and international security, make laws, and create institutions for insuring justice and freedom. In 1947 Winston Churchill said that democracy was "...the worst form of government except all those other forms that have been tried from time to time."[1]

Inefficiency is built in to any system that needs to get a consensus to move ahead. Athenian Democracy of 508 B.C. has stood for equality and freedom. Authoritarian political systems deny these principles and the politically strong impose their will on the politically weak. After the fall of Rome in 476 A.D., authoritarianism held sway for at least the next 700 years.

Magna Carta in 1215 might be given as the beginning of democratic forms. Magna Carta limited the power of the English King and gave various administrative powers to the land-owning nobles. For centuries previous to this, English kings often consulted with key advisors before making important proclamations concerning affairs of the realm such as taxes, defense, trade, petitions, and general matters of policy. Tribal assemblies in Nordic and Germanic societies to promote orderly and just interpersonal relations date to the 7th Century A.D. However, England was the first large country to develop a functional democratic system, constantly evolving over many centuries.

The word "parliament" used in the middle of the 13th century signified a formalization of this group of advisors, which gradually morphed into two chambers, The Houses of Lords and Commons. While the French king ruled by decree, the English king had to get approval from parliament for important policy decisions. Parliament even acquired the power of replacing the reigning king by the 14th century. Parliament even heard such mundane petitions as one peasant's complaint about a neighbor stealing his pig. Parliament became the high court of the realm.

Freedom, equality, justice, and security are the political jobs required in a nation which values humanistic principles. Order in society is perhaps the first responsibility of every government. Chaos leads to lawlessness and lawlessness can destroy the very fabric of Society. Somalia has been called a "Failed State," and roving bands of armed thugs control the streets and impose their will on powerless residents. This is civilization reduced to barbarism in which human dignity is subsumed in the "Law of the Jungle." Even international aid intended to relieve human suffering is diverted into the clutches of avaricious bullies. Under such conditions, improvement in the lives of the people cannot be achieved. A modern manifestation of Somalia's lawlessness and failure of its government to establish order and its descent into barbarism is the marauding bands of pirates along its coastline today.

War, natural disasters, foreign invasion, terrorism, criminal gangs, epidemic disease, riots, or similar societal upheaval can cause a government to lose control over its population and territory; order must be reestablished for any social improvements to take place. Tribalism and ethnic divisiveness also can lead to societal unrest and render government ineffective. The "Patria Chica" in Spain referred to the loyalty to local areas rather than to the national government. This problem bedeviled human well-being in Spain from the time of Columbus until modern times when Spain was admitted into the European Union.

Social order must be balanced against individual freedom for a nation to reach its full potential in human well-being. Government by the consent of the governed has the best opportunity to fulfill this seeming contradiction. In the most democratic of societies, there is always tension between freedom and social order. Most of us learned in political science 101 that although the First Amendment to the U.S. Constitution grants all citizens the right to "free speech," no one has the right to yell "fire" in a crowded theater in which there is no fire. We accept limits on free speech for the well-being of the society. The ACLU might argue that the right to free speech includes the right to disseminate pornography, while more conservative voices would argue that protecting society from harmful effects also must be considered. The ultimate arbitrator of conflicting government policies is a system in which people can change governments and philosophies on key issues with frequent and free elections. Pure democracy in which all citizens vote on all major issues can be realized only in small communities such as New England town meetings; representative democracies channel citizen's wishes into national policy through elected officials.

Governments are usually functionally divided into administrative, legislative, and judicial departments to perform the duties required of them. In a dictatorship, the executive might perform all functions and have no checks on decisions made. Civil servants are the professionals in government who run the everyday activities of such agencies as the post office, treasury, meteorological office, public health facilities, safety and security offices, transportation, national parks, international commerce and travel, military establishment, and many more. Civil servants are career workers and these jobs normally do not change hands when political parties change after elections. An honest and competent civil service in which promotions are based on good job performance is essential in promoting human well-being. Cronyism and bribes to get special favors done are sure signs of a corrupt political system in which human well-being is sacrificed to the benefit of special interests. Obviously, a good education system helps to promote a competent civil service.

Rich countries generally have a strong civil service sector, while poor countries have a civil service characterized by nepotism and privileges granted by illegal payments to government officials. Former British colonies such as India, Malaysia, Sri Lanka, Ghana, and Kenya emerged as independent nations with good civil service sectors because colonial governments trained local peoples in their duties. Yet another positive legacy from British colonialism is a strong school system which emphasized training in science and mathematics. Former French colonies such as Cambodia, Vietnam, Algeria, and Morocco did not fare so well because most colonial administrators were overseas Frenchmen. Training civil servants is an important task for many of the contemporary developing nations.

In like manner, legislators should be competent and willing to work for the human well-being of their constituents. Cases such as South Africa had legislators who catered to the needs of the white minority while making laws to subjugate the human well-being of the black majority. New nations with major ethnic or cultural divisions such as Iraq, Cyprus, Bolivia, Trinidad and Tobago, Nigeria, Northern Ireland, and Ethiopia can suffer from destructive competition as opposing groups try to secure their share of limited resources, sometimes at the disadvantage of other groups. In extreme cases, the competition can lead to civil war and the demise of a coherent nation or the emergence of dictatorial regimes. Another bromide from political science 101 is that the most difficult thing for a democracy to do is to defend itself democratically. In cases of extreme competition among diverse groups, human well-being can suffer long term losses.

As democratic national systems continue to evolve, legislators should channel the demands of their local citizens to the national level. Frequent free elections at national and local levels is the preferred system for insuring that citizen demands get heard, debated, and implemented as government policy. Political parties which represent various operational views and procedures are the instruments for articulating citizens' desires. Two parties seems to be the ideal in forming government's main policies for an elected term of office. Nations such as Italy, France, Germany, or Belgium have many party operatives with contrasting operational styles and philosophies. Sometimes this degenerates into a problem of forming a coherent and stable government. Parties not only represent major philosophies on the roles and operations of government, but they also mobilize the electorate in supporting various candidates for government positions.

Table 10.2 lists some 47 nations which are considered "Failed States." Such nations have dysfunctional political systems which fail to govern for the promotion of human well-being. Ironically in such dysfunctional nations, the military establishment is one of the few or only organized entities in the whole society. In turn, the military establishments are characterized by undemocratic hierarchal organization and strict obedience to orders from leaders downward. Democratic principles are sacrificed in such regimes.

Simon Bolivar was a general and leader in the independence movement of the South American countries from the colonial administration of Spain in the

Nineteenth Century. He believed that the new nations did not have the requisite institutions, especially educational levels, to underpin democratic political systems. His conclusion: the new nations would be better off with a paternalistic dictatorship until democratic institutions could be constructed. The problem with this approach is to find a truly paternalistic dictator and then trust that person to establish the appropriate democratic institutions.

After some 200 years of various types of dictatorships, most of the Latin American nations have finally segued, more or less, into political democracies. Chile, with the notable exception of the 1970s—1980s Pinochet dictatorship, is now among the handful of world nations that has full civil and political liberties. The United Nations was founded to foster peace, prosperity, human well-being, and the peaceful arbitration of disputes; in essence, the establishment of world-wide democratic nations.

Just like all other human systems, no government is perfect in providing its citizens with freedom, order, and justice. Freedom and order represent a tension because order requires the suppression of some freedoms; limited resources are opposed to unlimited demands on these resources; limited educational resources restrict the number and levels of education available to everyone; limited resources limit the amount of egalitarianism in society; governments have to extract resources from citizens to provide goods and services; limited resources require choices in investment for socio-economic improvement; choices have to be made to mete out justice; and changing technology requires governments to reexamine policies in their effectiveness in promoting human well-being.

Free and independent communications media is another vital set of institutions to enable democratic political systems. The people of a nation are the basis of all political legitimacy in democratic systems. Citizens need to have access to true information to make intelligent decisions to communicate their demands on government. Authoritative governments, on the other hand, control and distort information so that their citizens do not challenge government policies. Communications technology in rich countries has engendered information flow so prodigiously that there is almost too much information for people to digest. The internet, blogging, social networking, and evolving technology for sending and receiving information have raised the specter of the spread of rumors and false information. Ultimately, an intelligent and informed polity is necessary to insure order, freedom, and justice.

Freedomhouse is an international organization, funded mostly by the United States, which rates world nations annually on order, freedom, and justice. Its index ranges from 1 (perfectly free) to 7 (not free) on both civil liberties and political liberties. A total of 2 indicates free civil and political liberties, 14 indicates nations which have no freedom. We will use this indicator to determine which nations' political systems contribute to human well-being, and which do not. 1972 was the first date the index was published.

ENDNOTES

1. See: Churchill, Winston, "Speech to House of Commons," London, November 11, 1947.

Chapter Six
Overall Human Well-Being

It is clear that human well-being comes from all four systems: Physical, Social, Economic, and Political. Furthermore, all four systems interact in creating human well-being. How can we measure the impact of each system on the world's nations, and their combined effect? Because there are no direct measures of these systems, we will need to find surrogate measures with appropriate statistical approximations of their impact. Success in this endeavor should give us insight how rich or poor each nation is in each of the four systems, and then we need to estimate the effects of all systems in producing human well-being across the world. We use the word "indicators" rather than "measures" in order to convey the impression that whatever statistic chosen to represent a complex phenomenon will only be an approximation of the quality we are examining.

For the indicators of the physical environment and economic systems we have money data. Fortunately, statistics collectors such as the United Nations have adopted a measure called "Purchasing Power Parity" or PPP to express money values. PPP attempts to establish the value of a specific "basket of goods" in diverse nations to make comparisons among nations more valid from one nation to another and from one time period to another. To illustrate the concept, we can cite a somewhat facetious variant of this approach is to use a "big Mac" index to compare purchasing power in a variety of nations. This index calculates the cost of a McDonalds's sandwich to compare buying power in various nations.

To Recap Our Indicators: For the Physical System we have the total value of agriculture, forestry, and fishing production in one year to estimate the richness of a nation's physical environment. These are considered "renewable resources" that can sustain long-term output if properly managed. Elimination of mining from this output—a "non-renewable" industry—suppresses possible distortion of oil rich nations which may have no sustainable output from their physical system. In our tables, this output is expressed in PPP/capita. Gross Domestic Product is the usual measure of a nation's economic productivity. Defined as the market value of all goods and services produced in one year, again we use the PPP/capita for this statistic in economic tables. For the Physical and Economic Systems, we will evaluate the indicators for 1960 in rank order, the

2010 indicators in rank order, then we will compare the changes in values between 1960 and 2010 for seeking information about nations' progress.

The Social System is examined in terms of infant mortality rates. Infant mortality rates—the deaths of children less than one year old per 100,000 live births—imply many things about a nation's Social System. Educational attainment by parents, pre and post natal care, healthfulness of the physical environment, potability of the water supply, access to medical care, nutrition, general health of the pregnant mother, endemic and epidemic disease, cleanliness and amount of food supply, fertility of women, civil unrest, and many other characteristics of the Social System are reflected in infant mortality rates. The United Nation's agencies take careful statistics about the condition of the world's children in every nation. Therefore we can have reasonable confidence that the data are consistent and accurate.

Similar to our analysis in the other three national systems, we will seek information about the status and trends in infant mortality rates to evaluate the ability of the Social System to support human well-being in the world's nations. The wealth of a nation is important in the Social System as well as in the other three, but infant mortality rates add new insights about human well-being in the world's nations.

The Political System is difficult to evaluate. How can we assess a government's success or failure in providing its citizens with freedom, order, and justice? Fortunately, Freedom House, founded in the United States in 1941 to promote freedom and democracy around the world, rates civil liberties and political liberties in an annual report.[1] Supported by U.S. Government funds, Freedom House is a "non government organization (NGO)" which has offices in about a dozen countries. Using such variables as free and fair elections, effective collective bargaining, independent judiciary, free professional and private organizations, and the like, researchers rate countries from 1 (best) to 7 (worst) on civil liberties and political liberties. They combine scores on these two dimensions to rate a nation "free" or "not free." While the statistical validity of numbers derived from conclusions of "experts" has been challenged, this probably is the best available indicator of government effectiveness in providing freedom, order, and justice for its people. The limited range of numbers (1 to 7) for each factor means that many nations will have the same scores. We will cope with this problem in the chapter evaluating the Political Systems of each nation.

After each of the four systems is evaluated in terms of status and trends, we will aggregate the indicators to get a full picture of human well-being in the world's nations. A convenient and easy way to do this is to add the world rank of each nation on each factor to derive a score of overall human well-being. Then we can rank each nation from highest human well-being to lowest human well-being. This status ranking for 2010 will be followed by a ranking of each nation by trend, or the change in rankings from 1960 to 2010. This should give us insights about the characteristics of nations that have enjoyed progress in human well-being over the past 50 years compared to those which have failed to make much progress. Also it should point out whether or not the United Nations' Millennium Goals are being met. Perhaps this will help to point the way to improved progress in attaining human well-being in the world in the future.

The statistical universe in this book is the world's 151 nations that have populations of more than one million people. These vary in size from China's 1.33 billion to Timor L'Este's population of 1.1 million. Obviously, population size has an important impact on human well-being. A large population implies greater socio-economic diversity in all aspects of life, both positive and negative. More people means more labor to create goods and services, but they also create a large market for absorbing the output society creates. Small size means less economic productivity and less demand for the goods produced. The important point, first explained by Thomas Malthus, is that the productivity of the society must be greater than the population to have a growth in human well-being. The world of 2010 presents many nations in which population exceeds production and a growing number in which production far outstrips population growth. Our analysis of each nation's four systems should point out which nations are growing in human well-being and which are not. Furthermore, we hope to be able to uncover the major contributors that lead to success or failure.

For each of the Four Systems, a table in the Statistical Appendix (Tables Ap.1, Ap.2, Ap.3, and Ap.4) will list every nation's value on the given indicator in numerical order. In each chapter for each system, a table, (Tables 7.1, 8.1, 9.1, and 10.1) will list the nations whose scores record the greatest changes between 1960 and 2010, 1972 to 2010 for the Political System. Then we will examine a sampling of highest and lowest changes in individual nations scoring in our attempt to understanding the causes of high or low scores. This procedure should inform us of what has led to success in creating human well-being, and perhaps what must be done in the lagging nations to increase their human well-being.

ENDNOTES

1. See: Freedom House, www.freedomhouse.org/research.

Chapter Seven
World Physical Systems, Status and Trends

Tables 7.1 and Ap.1 (latter located in the Statistical Appendix) portray data about the world's Physical Systems. Perhaps the most important conclusion on this table (Ap.1) is the 144% growth in value-added in world agricultural output per capita between 1960 and 2010. Miracle wheat and miracle rice development illustrate the application of technological developments to agriculture and the benefits derived from it in increased food production. Remember that population grew by 125% during this time from about 3 billion to more than 6.9 billion. Pesticides, herbicides, fertilizer, improved plants, hydroponics, fish farming, forest management, irrigation, more scientific animal husbandry, and improved commercial fishing are the major technological inputs that have permitted the growth in crops, fishing, and forestry

The past 50 years has also seen the phenomenal growth in manufacturing and service industries. Today, agriculture produces only about 6% of the world's GDP.[1] Less than 11% of the world's land area is considered arable, and about 3 million square kilometers of land are irrigated. The land located along the humid/arid boundary, such as Africa's Sahel, Canada-U.S.A.'s Great Plains/Prairie, Russia's Steppes, and Australia's Murray-Darling region are subject to periodic drought. Long-term loss of agricultural land caused by desertification or land/grazing abuse, salinization, and erosion has recently become apparent in recent decades. Programs to prevent such disasters are being pursued. Conservation efforts in forestry and fishery management aim to produce sustainable output in these primary industries.

How are we going to feed future generations is a continuing concern to world leaders. Everyone has heard the story about population more than doubling between 1960 and 2010. Several rich nations such as Japan, most of the European Union, and South Korea have reached or almost reached zero population growth, but African, Asian, and some Latin American nations still have population growth rates in excess of 2%. The world as a whole has a population growth rate of more than 1.1%.[2] Conservation and programs such as the "Greening of the Environment" must continue to insure an adequate food supply, clean water, clear air, and an aesthetically pleasing Physical Environment for future generations.

Brazil, Madagascar, Indonesia, and a handful of other tropical nations believe that conservation is only a concern for rich nations; the first concern for poor nations is to feed and provide jobs for their growing populations. China and India have two of the most polluted physical environments in the world because both are hell-bent on raising the economic status of their huge populations and failing to invest much in conservation efforts. The recent earthquake and tsunami in Japan have threatened a major radiation emergency from leaks in a severely damaged nuclear plant. Some radiation from that plant reached the west coast of the United States in less than a week. Slowly, it seems, the entire world will realize that we are in a position in which we cannot risk environmental degradation if we expect the physical environment to provide human well-being for the foreseeable future.

Table Ap.1 in the Statistical Appendix lists the surprising fact that in 1960, the U.A.E. had by far the highest value-added per capita in agriculture of $1,257 (PPP), almost six times the world average. It was not until 1962 that the U.A.E. earned its first income from oil exports; most of the labor force was engaged in agriculture at that time. Nomadic herding was a major occupation. Dates, vegetables, poultry, fish, and meat were all produced by the small population of this recently formed nation. The result was a very high agricultural value-added per capita. Oil changed everything about the economy. U.A.E. now imports most of its food, paid for by oil exports, petro-chemicals, and a booming free trade zone. In 2010, U.A.E. ranked 108th in the world in value-added per capita from agriculture, and its $462 was only about two-thirds of the world average. Limited agricultural resources were more than compensated for by oil earnings, an industry based on a non-renewable resource. Having led the nation out of poverty, oil now presents the problem of creating industries that will outlast oil reserves.

Gabon, Papua N G, and Syria are somewhat surprising leaders in the agricultural value-added per capita in 1960. The others in the top 10% are westernized nations in which intensive inputs into agriculture support high output of vegetables, fruits, fish, meat, dairy products, and forest products. Gabon and Papua N G even today have populations of 2 and 6 million respectively that can be supported by their physical environment for producing tropical products. Many tropical agricultural products are industrial inputs. Timber and manganese exports were important industries in 1960, and then offshore oil and natural gas came into production for Gabon, giving this country more money to invest in agriculture. Papua N G has abundant natural resources, but they are difficult to exploit because of rugged terrain, tropical rainforest, and adverse tropical climate characteristics. Under Australian colonial rule, tropical hardwoods, and a variety of tropical agricultural products were produced for export. Gabon got its independence from France in 1960 and Papua N G got its independence from Australia in 1975. Thus the legacy of two rich nations helped develop agricultural output up to 1960.

Table 7.1

Change in Agricultural Value Added Per Capita, 1960-2010
Constant Dollars (PPP)

Rank	Country	1960—2010	1960	2010
1	Ireland	1,944	166	2,110
2	Denmark	1,344	312	1,656
3	Iran	1,276	130	1,406
4	Serbia	1,112	209	1,321
5	Malaysia	1,082	413	1,495
6	Albania	949	349	1,298
7	Thailand	899	97	996
8	Slovakia	891	169	1,060
9	Armenia	858	239	1,097
10	Macedonia	839	232	1,071
11	Chad	813	102	915
12	Belarus	812	267	1,079
13	Uruguay	800	407	1,207
14	Australia	789	685	1,474
86	U.S.A.	278	279	557
138	Sweden	81	508	589
139	Germany	80	227	307
140	Afghanistan	78	170	248
141	Congo Zaire	66	99	165
142	Burundi	57	43	100
143	Georgia	54	478	532
144	Trinidad & Tobago	44	72	116
145	Eritrea	38	83	121
146	Oman	25	477	502
147	Mauritania	-2	265	263
148	Zimbabwe	-118	137	19
149	Switzerland	-328	828	500
150	Japan	-422	944	522
151	U.A.E.	-795	1,257	462
			Mean = 279	*Mean = 638*

Source: Table Ap.1, Statistical Appendix

Table 7.2

Population Density Versus Food Growing Capacity

Rank	Nation	Population	Density/Arable Land
151	Australia	21,515,754	43
150	Kazakhstan	15,460,484	69
149	Canada	33,759,742	78
148	Niger	15,878,271	84
147	Russia	139,390,205	117
146	Lithuania	3,545,319	123
145	Latvia	2,217,969	128
144	Argentina	41,343,201	144
143	Ukraine	45,415,596	145
142	Belarus	9,612,632	177
141	U.S.A.	310,232,863	179
140	Paraguay	6,375,830	214
139	Zambia	12,056,923	215
138	Hungary	9,880,059	219
137	Cent Af Rep	4,844,927	219
1	Singapore	4,701,069	440,998
2	Kuwait	2,759,132	15,603
3	Oman	2,967,717	11,780
4	U.A.E.	4,975,593	6,404
5	Qatar	840,926	4,601
6	S.Korea	48,636,068	2,988
7	Taiwan	23,024,956	2.932
8	Japan	126,804,433	2,924
9	Egypt	80,471.869	2,668
10	Papua N G	6,064,515	2,503
11	Lebanon	4,125,247	2,290
12	Sri Lanka	21,513,990	2,269
13	Netherlands	16,783,092	2,205
14	Israel	7,353,985	2,147
15	Colombia	44,205,293	2,064

Source: CIA World Factbook 2011

All three of these nations have fallen somewhat in world rankings in 2010. U.A.E.'s agricultural value-added per capita in 2010 is $462 which earns a world ranking of 108 out of 151 nations. U.A.E.'s agricultural output is now less than the world average. Oil, petrochemicals, construction, and trade now account for most of the nation's investment and poor agricultural resources can almost be ignored as food imports take the place of domestically produced food.

Service industries such as banking and tourism will probably see the most development in the near term.

Papua N G has abundant mineral resources, and the nation is now concentrating on developing these rather than depend on agriculture, forestry, and fishing. The country ranks 38th in Physical System productivity in 2010, with a value-added per capita of $782, which is slightly above the world average. Agriculture is divided into a large subsistence sector, and a much smaller, but growing export sector. Some 85% of workers are employed in farming, but the sector produces only about one-third of GDP. Government investments encourage export crops of sugar cane, coffee, cacao, tea, rubber, and oil palm. Foreign investment concentrates on oil, natural gas, and mineral resources. Papua N G's Physical System seems to presage a good balanced exploitation (positive sense) of its natural resources.

Agriculture has played a leading role in the Syrian economy for 10,000 years, because here is where the original Agricultural Revolution—the domestication of plants and animals—took place. Mediterranean climate in the north and irrigation from the Euphrates Valley and its tributaries have created the conditions for agriculture, the leading economic enterprise until the 1970s. Water disputes with Turkey, drying up wetlands for urban uses, and overuse of irrigation have degraded the physical environment somewhat. Agriculture, including a small forest products industry, produces about 19% of the nation's GDP. The most important export crop is cotton, a slightly inferior product compared to Egypt's extra long staple variety. Wheat, barley, olives, fruit, tobacco, chickpeas, poultry, and dairy products serve the local market and some are exported. Some food and livestock must be imported. Syria's value- added per capita from agriculture in 1960 was $519, ranking the country 12th in the world, while its $874 in 2010 ranked the country 26th in the world. Fishing is a relatively underdeveloped sector.

Agriculture in Mediterranean and other dry climates presents many hazards. Periodic drought, land destruction, invasions of crop eating insects, and decreasing fertility of fragile soils require careful management and investment in physical resources. A population growth rate of almost 2% means that population will double in only 35 years. Small and declining oil production and the agricultural limitations will likely mean that Syria will try to become less dependent on its physical environment in the future.

African nations, Afghanistan, Yemen, Jordan, Kuwait, Trinidad and Tobago, and Singapore have the world's lowest value-added per capita from agriculture according to Table Ap.1, in 2010. All these nations record GDP from agriculture of about one-third of the world average. Political instability has sabotaged the development of these African nations. In 1960, the Belgian Congo was a thriving mining economy, with copper, oil, uranium, gold, silver, diamonds, coal, zinc, cobalt, and other minerals feeding the European economy. Most of the investment in infrastructure was devoted to these industries and very little went to utilize the great agricultural and forestry resources. Corrupt governments, civil war, and foreign invaders kept the cycle of poverty going into today's underdeveloped status of Congo Zaire. Similar experiences were suffered by Eritrea, Burundi, Guinea, Zimbabwe, Mozambique, and Mauritania. All these nations which rank in the lower 10% of the world's nations in value-added per capita in agriculture have substantial resources in their Physical Systems. Lack of infrastructure and investment in modern technology to make these resources productive keeps production from the physical environment artificially low. These nations could produce large amounts of foodstuffs if such investments would be applied. International aid has been ineffective for many reasons, probably with ineffective governments being the most serious. Afghanistan, Yemen, Congo Zaire, Eritrea, Zimbabwe, and Burundi are all on Table 10.2, the Failed States Index. Fifty years of little progress dims the prospects for future development.

The United States ranks 86th in the world with $557 of value-added per capita from agriculture in 2010. A scant 1.2% of GDP is derived from primary industries in the U.S.A. and in the past 25 years, little investment has been put into agriculture, fishing, and forestry. Agricultural products comprise more than 9% of exports and about 5% of imports. Traditionally, the U.S.A. has had surpluses of corn, cotton, wheat, and meat; also farm subsidies such as the "soil bank" has paid farmers NOT to produce food. Clearly the United States could produce much more in agricultural products if there was a demand to do so. Recent conservation efforts are aimed at cleaning the air, water, and preserving the natural condition of the forests.

The productivity of the physical environment for the world's rich nations is far below what could be produced, because the economic emphasis on manufacturing and services means a de-emphasis on production from the physical environment. Table 7.2 shows the population density compared to arable land. Australia has only 43 people per acre of arable land, while Singapore has 440,998. These of course are extreme cases. All the rest of the nations listed on the upper part of Table 7.2 have population density compared to arable land per capita of less than 220. All of the nations on the bottom half of Table 7.2 have population densities of more than 2,200 per arable acre. The latter represent the overpopulation—ratio of people per farmland—and the diminished food production possibilities of desert, crowded Asian, and crowded small Western European economies. Obviously South Korea, Japan, and the Netherlands have such productive manufacturing and service economies that this "overpopulation" is not a problem. For the others, all of which have population growth rates that average about 2%, must be concerned with the Malthusian Theorem of population growth outstripping the ability to produce food to sustain them. Unfortunately, many if not most of the world's poor nations are in this position.

Another lens from which to view the "richness of the environment" is to consider the effects of environment destruction. Conservation of the environment has become a great concern in recent decades as the world's people have become aware of the more than doubling of the world's population between 1960 and 2010. Issues such as global warming, water pollution, air pollution, soil depletion, acid rainfall, and energy depletion have become hot topics for international discussion, but also as topics for international treaties and efforts to "save the planet." Table 7.3 is merely a glimpse of the air pollution problem. The United Nations World Health Organization (WHO) estimates that 1.6 million people die each year (one per every 20 seconds) from breathing indoor air pollution.

The data on Table 7.3 is a brief selection from a report by the World Bank Development Research Group and Environmental Department. These organizations take air samplings from selected stations in the world's major cities. Particulates, sulfur dioxide, and nitrogen dioxide are reported in the listed cities. Particulates are solid matter such as soot, wind-blown sand and salt, and incineration of wood, dung, charcoal—all cooking fuels of the poor -; sulfur dioxide is a chemical compound produced by volcanoes and industrial processes; nitrogen dioxide is a chemical compound diffused into the atmosphere by internal combustion engines, power stations, and other engines and industrial processes. The latter two can produce acid rainfall which threatens vegetation and soil productivity.

Some 24 Chinese cities in all parts of the country were listed in these data (only 7 listed here). Seventeen of them had particulates values far above the world mean; twenty one had sulfur dioxide levels far above the world mean; and thirteen had nitrogen dioxide levels above the world mean.

Table 7.3
Air Pollution in Major Cities of the World in Micrograms/Cu Meter

City	Particulates	Sulfur Dioxide	Nitrogen Dioxide
Cairo, Egypt	169	69	-
Delhi, India	150	24	41
Calcutta, India	128	49	34
Tianjin, China	125	82	50
Chungking, China	123	340	70
Kanpur, India	109	15	14
Lucknow, India	109	26	25
Jakarta, Indonesia	104	-	-
Zhengzhow, China	97	63	95
Jinan, China	94	132	45
Lanzhou, China	91	102	104
Beijing, China	89	90	122
Taiyuan, China	88	211	55
Ahmadabad, India	83	30	21
Bangkok, Thailand	79	11	23
Sofia, Bulgaria	61	39	122
Santiago, Chile	61	29	81
Tehran, Iran	58	209	-
London, U.K.	21	25	77
Paris, France	11	14	57

City	Particulates	Sulfur Dioxide	Nitrogen Dioxide
Berlin, Germany	22	18	26
Chicago, U.S.A.	25	14	57
Los Angeles, U.S.A.	34	9	74
New York, U.S.A.	21	26	79
World Means:	48	46	45

Source: Selected data from World Bank Development Research Group and Environmental Department

Sulfur Dioxide and Nitrogen Dioxide can lead to Acid Rain

Chungking (Chongking) had by far the world's most polluted atmosphere. China's rapid modern industrialization and use of coal as a major fuel for energy production and India's large population, most of whom are very poor, and its huge stock of cattle, also contribute mightily to world air pollution. India has also been industrializing, again using coal as a major energy source. These conditions—huge populations and rapid industrialization—are distinct threats to the sustainability of their physical environments. With the exception of Eastern Europe's Bulgaria, Western Europe, and the U.S.A. have manageable problems of environmental degradation. The U.S.A. still has the problem of pollution from internal combustion of its many automobiles. The cases of Egypt, Indonesia, Thailand, and Iran are worrisome because they are large nations attempting rapid economic growth. The United Nations will have to lead the way if responsible economic development is to occur.

Thus our Table 7.1 conclusions about human well-being from changes in agricultural value-added per capita between 1960 and 2010 must recognize the complexity of the problem of productivity of the Physical System. Obviously the nations with highest growth in agricultural value-added have excellent physical resources. The nations at the lower end of this table, however, include nations with poor physical resources and nations which have put major emphasis on industrial and service growth at the expense of agriculture. Their high income means that they can import meat, fruits and vegetables, and forest products from other parts of the world more cheaply. No indicator of complex systems will ever be perfect, but our indicator of the growth of value-added in agriculture gives us a good start in evaluating human well-being among the world's nations which vary so widely in human development and their prospects for attaining higher levels of human well-being.

ENDNOTES

1. See: CIA, World Factbook 2011, New York: Skyhorse Publishing, 2010.

2. CIA, Ibid.

Chapter Eight
World Social Systems, Status and Trends

The Social System comprises all personal interactions from joining a family at birth; through joining a kindergarten class; through joining the Red Sox Nation; through joining the workforce; through marriage and raising a family; through joining a professional organization or political party; to joining a bereavement group at the death of a spouse. All Social Systems need to have organizations to promote individual skills, education, and training to socialize young people into the nation's social structure. In like manner, organizations should exist to create cooperative associations of individuals who share similar interests, whether they be educational, recreational, political, economic, or others. Social cohesion and opportunities for individual social growth are important to overcome the inevitable class divisions which arise in a society because of differing occupations, incomes, intellectual attainment, and many other factors. The ideal society should minimize destructive competition among classes of people by providing equal opportunity for upward social mobility based on merit and attainment. The artificial "workers' paradise" of the Communist Countries have now been thoroughly discredited, in theory and practice.

> In fact, Danes have more in common with Jamaicans when it comes to tolerating ambiguity than they do with some of their European peers. Denmark and Belgium may share in a kind of broad European liberal-democratic tradition, but they have different histories, different political structures, different religious traditions, and different languages and food and architecture and literature—going back hundreds and hundreds of years. And the sum total of all those differences is that in certain kinds of situations that require dealing with risk and uncertainty, Danes tend to react in a very different way from Belgians.[1]

Religion, ethnic-tribal divisions, economic classes, workers guilds, competition for limited resources, especially land, are historically important divisive elements in societies. Diversity has been celebrated in multi-cultural societies such as that of the United States. Whereas the former "melting pot" ideal of molding diversity into a new culture of assimilation used to exist, the new concept of a "salad bowl" in which a new society is created in which individuality is retained has yet to prove itself in a smooth functioning nation. Japan disagrees with the "salad bowl" concept of social cohesion. The world history of Social Systems functionality seems to agree with the Japanese.

The world of 2010 abounds in examples to support a "melting pot" concept of societies which are to have Social Systems which promote human well-being. The Israeli-Palestinian conflict; the former Catholic-Protestant conflict in Northern Ireland; the Kurd-Iraqi-Turkey-Iran conflict; the Tutsi-Hutu conflict in Rwanda and Burundi; the former Africaaner-African conflict in South Africa; the quiet Celtic-French conflict in Normandy and Brittany; the conflict between Basques and Spaniards in Spain; the Shiite-Sunni conflict in Iraq; Turks vs. Greeks in Cyprus; Serbs-Croats in Serbia; Russians and Georgians in former Soviet Union; Indios and Ladinos in Bolivia; Montagnards and Vietnamese in Vietnam, and the Uigurs and Chinese in China illustrate the universality of social conflict. The list could obviously be much longer. Religion, ethnicity, territory, past atrocities, educational, financial, and world view differences make for divisiveness in society. Somehow, societal homogeneity and competition among these differences must be forged to develop a society in which there is abundant human well-being for everyone. Iceland, Finland, Sweden, Norway, Denmark, and Japan lead nearly every index ever created to measure human well-being. All of these nations have cultural homogeneity.

Variations in infant mortality rates are key indicators about cooperation among people, and therefore they represent the degree of human well-being in nations around the world. As stated above, infant mortality rates describe many aspects of society that either add to or detract from human well-being. Low ratios imply healthy mothers, normal birth weights, good education of parents, good pre natal and post natal care, availability of doctors, medicines, and medical facilities, good nutrition, clean water, good sanitation, lack of endemic and epidemic disease, order in society, good networks of support for parents and children, and safe homes and equipment for raising young children. High infant mortality rates suggest opposite conditions in such afflicted nations. No simple index can accurately describe the full implications of complex conditions that promote social cohesion, individual social growth, and human well-being from the Social System. However, the variations in infant mortality rates among the world's nations, status and trends will give us a clear signal about which nations have productive Social Systems and which unfortunate nations do not. AIDS is a modern curse that has boosted infant mortality rates in many nations. World Health Organization estimates place the number of people in the world that are living with the AIDS virus at 33 million. Many African nations suffer from high rates of infection.

Table Ap.2 in the Statistical Appendix lists all 151 of the world's nations, their infant mortality rates for 1960 and for 2010, and the progress in reducing these numbers over the past 50 years. Perhaps the most important fact revealed in Table Ap.2 is the world's overall decrease in infant mortality rates from an average of 113 in 1960 to 30 in 2010. While this is good news about the improvement in human well-being in general, it also raises the spectre of a population boom in nations that can least afford such a circumstance. It also suggests the sad fact that even in 2010, 40% of the world's nations have infant mortality rates above the world average and that the lowest 33 nations have twice the world average in infant mortality. Haiti, Burundi, Ethiopia, Sudan, Somalia, Niger, Afghanistan, and Angola are virtually synonymous with human misery in all its dimensions.

Table 8.1 shows the change in infant mortality rates over the past 50 years. All the nations experiencing low change since 1960, except Zambia, are universally recognized to be in the group of the world's highly developed nations, the European Union and related nations. Zambia's low absolute change is a statistical anomaly, resulting from a high rate in 1960 and a lower, but still very high rate in 2010. All the other nations with low infant mortality rate changes had strong Social Systems in 1960 and even more human well-being from their Social Systems in 2010. The case of the United States is an interesting one. Its infant mortality rate of 26 infant deaths per 100,000 live births in 1960 placed this nation 11th in the world (See: Table Ap.2 in the Statistical Appendix). Its rate of 6 in 2010 placed it 28th in the world, a significant absolute rate of decline, but not significant relative to the decline in other nations. Part of the explanation for this statistical decline is the rapid improvement in the world's rich countries. However, it is impossible to ignore the conclusion that the world's third most populous nation has developed a large and growing underclass.

Table 8.2 shows human well-being in the European Union. Greece, Spain, and Portugal were relatively poor nations in 1960. For some 1500 years after the fall of Rome, Europe was politically fragmented into many competing political units and groups. Tribal, territorial, ethnic, language, religious, historical experiences, economic classes, revenge, royal succession, and world views and many other factors led to almost constant turmoil and bloodshed. After the devastation of two world wars fought mostly within Europe, complete with great physical destruction and societal upheaval, post World War II Europe embarked on efforts to end the conflicts and seek cooperative efforts. The result is the European Union. The improvements in human well-being of Greece, Spain, and Portugal can be directly attributed to their having to initiate social, economic, and political reforms to join the union. The same is true for the Eastern European nations after the collapse of the Soviet Union. In spite of the failures of ASEAN, LAFTA, CAFTA, CARIFTA, the African Union, and other regional organizations up to this time, it appears that some form of international formal cooperation is the only chance the poor countries of 2010 have if they are to improve the human well-being in these countries.

Table 8.1
Change in Infant Mortality Rates, 1960- 2010

Rank	Country	Change	1960	2010
1	Netherlands	13	18	5
2	Sweden	13	16	3
3	Norway	15	19	4
4	Australia	15	20	5
5	New Zealand	17	22	5
6	Finland	18	22	4
7	Czech Rep	18	22	4
8	Switzerland	18	22	4
9	Denmark	18	22	4
10	U.K.	18	23	5
11	U.S.A.	20	26	6
12	Canada	23	28	5
13	Zambia	25	126	101
14	Slovakia	26	33	7
15	Latvia	26	35	9
138	Gambia	138	207	69
139	Somalia	141	250	109
140	Azerbaijan	145	200	55
141	Tunisia	147	170	23
142	Oman	147	164	17
143	Eritrea	148	191	43
144	Guinea	150	215	65
145	Chad	151	250	99
146	Turkmenistan	155	200	45
147	Saudi Arabia	158	170	12
148	Egypt	159	186	27
149	Timor L'Este	159	200	41
150	Nepal	164	212	48
151	Mali	169	285	116

1960 Mean = 113, 2010 Mean = 30

Source: Table Ap.2, Statistical Appendix, (rates are per 100,000 live births)

Consider the data on Table 8.3, Social Structures of the World's Largest Nations. China has 39.9 million people below its poverty level. (It should be noted that each nation defines its own poverty level, and this low figure for China—3% -is obviously too low). India has almost the population of the United States it considers its underclass. With low GDP per capita, the "middle class" in poor countries would probably be considered the underclass in rich nations. Nevertheless, relative conditions of underprivileged status puts stress on social cohesion and social human well-being in nations. 37 million in the lower class in the U.S.A. raises many social, economic, and political strains on the society. The recent recession and loss of more than 7 million jobs, foreclosure on millions of homes, and new educational requirements for new job openings will create basic changes in social structure of the U.S.A. even just to maintain the social human well-being that now exists. Governments must have the ability to recognize significant societal changes from whatever source that threaten human well-being and be able to devise policies to eliminate the threat. Countries can slide backward, as well as progress. China's recent rapid economic growth undoubtedly will leave a large segment of the population behind and require social, economic, and maybe even political adjustments to maintain social peace. Governments must be ever vigilant in the modern world to keep their countries on the constant path to improvement in human well-being.

> True, 200 million of China's subjects, fortunate to work for an expanding global market, are increasingly enjoying a middle-class standard of living. The remaining one billion, however, are among the poorest and most exploited people in the world, lacking even minimal rights and public services. The Party, while no longer totalitarian, is still cruel and oppressive.[2]

Table 8.2
Change in Infant Mortality Rates, 1960- 2010

Rank	Country	Join	Pop	% Urban	Lit	Yrs Ed	GDP/C
1	Germany	orig	82.3	74	99	16.0	$34,100
2	France	orig	64.1	77	99	16.5	32,800
3	U.K.	orig	61.3	90	99	16.5	35,200
4	Italy	orig	58.1	68	98	16.5	30,300
5	Spain	1986	40.5	77	98	16.5	33,700
6	Poland	2004	38.5	61	100	15.5	17,900
7	Romania	2007	22.2	54	98	14.0	11,500
8	Netherlands	orig	16.8	82	99	16.5	39,200
9	Portugal	1986	10.7	59	93	15.5	21,800
10	Greece	1981	10.8	61	96	17.0	32,100
11	Belgium	orig	10.4	97	99	16.0	36,600
12	Czech Rep	2004	10.2	73	99	15.0	25,100
13	Hungary	2004	9.9	68	99	15.5	18,600
14	Sweden	1995	9.1	85	99	16.0	36,800
15	Austria	1995	8.2	67	98	15.5	39,400
16	Bulgaria	2007	7.1	71	98	13.5	12,600
17	Denmark	1973	5.5	87	99	16.5	36,000
18	Slovakia	2004	5.5	56	100	14.5	21,200
19	Finland	1995	5.3	63	100	17.5	34,900
20	Ireland	1973	4.3	61	99	17.5	42,200
21	Lithuania	2004	3.6	67	100	16.0	15,400
22	Latvia	2004	2.2	68	100	15.5	14,500
23	Slovenia	2004	2.0	48	100	16.5	27,900
24	Estonia	2004	1.3	69	100	16.0	18,700
25	Cyprus	2004	1.1	70	98	13.5	21,200
26	Luxembourg	orig	.5	82	100	13.5	78,000
27	Malta	2004	.4	94	93	15.0	23,800

Join = Year joined (orig = original members); Pop = Population; Urban = % urbanized; Liter = % Literate; yrs ed = average years of education; GDP = Gross Domestic Product per Capita.

Table 8.3
Social Structures of the World's Largest Nations

Rank	Nation	Pop (Mil)	Life	Below 15	Lit	Under	GDP/C
1	China	1,330	75	18	91	3	$6,600
2	India	1,173	66	30	61	25	3,100
3	U.S.A.	310	78	20	99	12	46,400
4	Indonesia	243	71	28	90	18	4,000
5	Brazil	201	72	27	89	26	10,200
6	Pakistan	177	65	36	50	24	2,600
7	Bangladesh	158	60	34	48	36	1,600
8	Nigeria	152	47	41	68	70	2,400
9	Russia	139	66	15	99	16	15,100
10	Japan	127	82	13	99	13	32,600
11	Mexico	112	76	29	91	18	13,500
12	Philippines	100	71	35	93	33	3,300
13	Vietnam	90	72	26	90	12	2,900
14	Ethiopia	88	56	46	43	39	900
15	Germany	82	79	14	99	11	34,100
16	Egypt	80	72	33	71	20	6,000
17	Turkey	78	72	27	87	17	11,200
18	Congo Zaire	71	55	47	67	70	300
19	Iran	67	71	21	77	18	12,900
20	Thailand	66	73	20	93	10	8,100
21	France	64	81	19	99	6	32,800
22	U.K.	61	79	17	99	14	35,200
23	Italy	58	80	13	98	6	30,300
24	Myanmar	53	65	28	90	33	1,100
25	S. Africa	49	49	29	86	50	10,100
26	S. Korea	49	79	16	98	15	28,000

Pop (Mil) = Population in millions; Life = Life Expectancy at Birth; Below 15 = % Population Below 15 Years Old; Lit = Literacy Rate; Under = % of Population Below Poverty Level; GDP/C = Gross Domestic Product Per Capita

ENDNOTES

1. Gladwell, Malcom, *Outliers: The Story Of Success*, New York: Little Brown and Company, 2008, p. 204.

2. Sorman, Guy, "The Truth About China," The Wall Street Journal, Friday, April 22, 2007.

Chapter Nine
World Economic Systems, Status and Trends

Economic development programs traditionally concentrate early improvements in the Economic System. The reasons for this are the following: 1. Economic systems are the easiest to analyze; 2. Projects to increase the production of goods and services are the easiest to devise; 3. Economic output can be raised quickly, and 4. Economic change can be expected to lead to social and political improvements in human well-being in the long run. Such development philosophies have been tried in Southeast Asia, Africa, and Latin America, but success has come only slowly and only in selected cases.

> The fact that America has shied away from seeking vast geopolitical transformations has often associated it with defense of the traditional, and sometimes the political, status quo. Trusting in the rule of law, it has found it difficult to recognize its faith in peaceful change with the historical fact that almost all significant changes in history have involved violence and upheaval.[1]

The fact that economic development of most of the rich nations of 2010 took many decades to achieve should not be taken as the only way 2010's poor nations can experience sustained and substantial economic growth. Today capital, management, technology, raw materials and semi-finished parts, labor, and even markets are readily mobile over the surface of the globe. Witness the rapid economic rise of China, India, Brazil, Russia, Taiwan, and South Korea. Today, cheap labor as in the case of China, well-trained engineers in India, great natural resources of Brazil and Russia, and hard-working and disciplined workforces in Taiwan and South Korea are irresistible draws for international capital, branch manufacturing, and the supply of semi-finished goods for assembly into more complex products. Globalization is the new stimulus for developing a productive manufacturing sector in a number of countries where political stability and social cohesion can attract big name manufacturers.

> The biggest upside is that Globalization is bringing more and more people out of poverty faster than ever before in the history of the world. The biggest downside is that in raising standards of living, Globalization is making possible much higher levels of production and consumption by many more people.[2]

Primary industries—those in which natural resources play a pivotal role in the production process—are important in all economies, even the sophisticated manufacturing nations. Kuwait, U.A.E., Saudi Arabia, Iran, Iraq, Nigeria, and Trinidad and Tobago derive most of their national incomes from oil. Oil is still the world's most important energy source, driving machinery, automobiles, power plants, ships, aircraft, and factories. Oil also provides raw materials for the petrochemical industry which makes everything from fertilizer to plastics. Many nations have become wealthy from oil revenues. However, oil is a non-renewable resource and its exploitation and uses cause major environmental pollution. The mining industry produces gold, silver, gem stones, building materials, metals, and numerous other useful products.

Agriculture, animal husbandry, fishing, and forestry were the first industries to feed, clothe, and shelter humankind, and they remain basic components to sustain modern nations. Most of the world's farmers today are engaged in subsistence agriculture, growing only enough to feed their families and perhaps a little surplus for sale to local markets. On the other end of the agriculture scale, "factories in the fields" are large scale operations utilizing high capital and technological inputs to feed the masses in industrial societies. Fishing has a similar structure, as does animal husbandry and forestry. While primary economic activities add substantial income to many nations, there is no modern nation in the world that has become highly developed based on agriculture or mining alone.

The Industrial Revolution of the early 19th century began the process of creating highly productive, rich societies. Manufacturing has a great variety of production processes, ranging from the simple manufacture of textiles to the highly complex manufacture of medical machinery and pharmaceuticals. In fact the great variety of manufacturing types means that large amounts of capital, technology, and highly trained workers can produce an infinity of products, limited only by the market's desire to consume these products. Thus the manufacturing economy can expand prodigiously. England, France, Germany, Belgium, the Netherlands, Italy, the United States, Japan, South Korea, and Taiwan and other nations have used this model of economic growth, starting with textile and other simple manufactures, gradually working their way up to the manufacturing of highly engineered products such as automobiles. This is a sound path to higher productivity and higher incomes.

Tertiary economic activities always include the skills of workers, from selling vacuum cleaners door to door, to research for products in the bio-medical engineering field. Some economists insist that there is a "Quaternary Sector" which is made up of banking and finance; for simplicity, we will include this important sector in Tertiary Industries. International money flows, both legal and illegal, are a dominant element in the world's Economic System today. Switzerland, with a total GDP (PPP) of $317 billion and a per capita GDP (PPP) of $41,700, holds one-third of all the world's "offshore capital," estimated at 4 trillion U.S. dollars in 2010. 3 Employing more than 195,000 at home, the nation has numerous branch banks in other nations.

Swiss banking secrecy dates to the Middle Ages and it is based on the philosophy of the sacredness of people's privacy. So as not to be required to open up its banking practices, Switzerland has not joined the European Union and only became a member of the United Nations in 2002. Particularly controversial are the Swiss numbered accounts for which no information about the owner will be revealed. Other nations worry that their citizens might use such accounts to avoid taxes and to conceal illegally acquired money. Another serious concern is the anonymity of international terrorists hiding money meant to fund their dirty operations, such as drug trafficking, funding of criminal activities, defrauding tax authorities, and funding terrorism. The Cayman islands, Panama, Singapore, and virtually all other rich countries have international banks; it is estimated that such banks have assets in excess of $96 trillion dollars, which is about 1.4 times the GDP of the entire world.

Research and development is another highly productive Tertiary Industry. Innovation in the modern age is a powerful mechanism for generating economic growth. Major discoveries of course cause sea changes for humanity, but even small changes in useful products can make life safer, healthier, happier, and more profitable. A nation's research takes place in private research institutes, government laboratories, universities, company laboratories, and garages. An educated and enterprising population is the essential element. Comparison of the Sears Roebuck catalogues of 1911 and 2011 might well be a showroom for innovation (pick any extensive catalog you wish). The world's rich nations average 73% of their labor forces employed in Tertiary Industries. In addition to the above, the tertiary also includes such productive activities as medicine, education, engineering, law, government, entertainers, and managers of every type.

Table 9.1
Changes in GDP/CAPITA (PPP), 1960-2010

Rank	Country	Change	1960	2010
1	Singapore	$58,774	$3,426	$62,200
2	Norway	46,591	12,509	51,900
3	Taiwan	33,420	1,680	35,100
4	U.S.A.	32,026	15,374	47,400
5	Ireland	31,475	6,125	37,600
6	Austria	30,216	10,284	40,300
7	U.A.E.	30,200	10,000	40,200
8	Japan	28,200	5,489	34,200
9	S. Korea	28,687	1,513	30,200
10	Netherlands	28,258	12,242	40,500
11	Belgium	27,823	10,077	37,900
12	Sweden	27,817	11,183	39,000
13	Canada	26,899	12,701	39,000
14	Finland	26,737	8,563	35,300

Rank	Country	Change	1960	2010
15	Spain	25,194	4,306	29,500
137	Zambia	-41	1,514	1,500
138	Afghanistan	-69	869	800
139	Burundi	-97	397	300
140	Togo	-111	1,011	900
141	Liberia	-145	645	500
142	Sierra Leone	-181	1,081	900
143	Niger	-203	903	700
144	Zimbabwe	-427	527	100
145	Haiti	-481	1,781	1,300
146	Cent Af Rep	-525	1,225	700
147	Congo Zaire	-574	874	300
148	Madagascar	-638	1,638	1,000
149	Somalia	-704	1,304	600
150	Iraq	-3,901	7,501	3,600
151	Kuwait	-42,563	94,000	51,700
	1960 World Mean = $4,384	*2010 World Mean = $12,575*		

Source: Table Ap.3, Statistical Appendix

Table Ap.3 in the Statistical Appendix shows all 151 nations and their GDP/Capita (PPP) for 1960 and 2010, while Table 9.1, shows the 10% of nations which record the greatest growth during the past 50 years and the bottom 10% which have had the lowest growth. Taiwan, Singapore, Spain, Japan, South Korea, Greece, and Ireland scored the most remarkable growth based on sustained increases in all aspects of their economies. Singapore, more properly considered a "city state" rather than a nation, capitalized on its traditional role as a major entrepot for the expanding economies of south, southeast, and east Asia. Its industrialization under a somewhat despotic political system, good social order, a well trained and educated workforce, international finance, and other factors raised human well-being from the Economic System substantially in these 50 years. Taiwan, South Korea, and Japan developed phenomenal economic growth with military and financial aid from the United States. Guaranteeing their international security, the United States freed these nations from heavy defense costs in a volatile part of the world. Reinvestment of earnings, a disciplined and obedient labor force, technological inputs from the U.S.A., and markets in the U.S. all combined for a dynamic program of economic growth and prosperity.

All the other nations experiencing rapid economic growth during the past 50 years also received direct and indirect support from the United States. The Marshall Plan after World War II gave impetus to the economic resurgence of Europe after the devastation of the war. It took only until about 1947 for Europe to regain pre-war productivity, a modern economic miracle. Formation of the European Union and NATO were other significant factors facilitating European prosperity. Canada is the United States' greatest trading partner; the longest unguarded international border in the world; and vast physical resources are all important reasons for Canadian superlative economic growth. Special trade relationships with the U.S., dynamic diversification of oil revenues, and a vibrant free trade zone has brought the U.A.E. into the modern world of high economic human well-being; and this was done from a start in 1960 as a backward region of nomads, sharply limited resources, and a disorganized, old fashioned government.

The bottom half of Table 9.1, mostly reveals nations with very low and declining human well-being from the Economic System. Kuwait is the exceptional case, its low ranking on this table stemming from extraordinary wealth in 1960 from oil revenues, and mere wealth from oil revenues in 2010. Kyrgyzstan, Moldova, Uzbekistan, and Tajikistan were all parts of the Soviet Union in 1960. Having no individual statistical identity, they were assigned Russia's GDP/Capita of $4,000 for 1960. Moldova is an impoverished bit of Europe with few resources and great dependence on Russia and the Ukraine. Attempting to join the European Union, Moldova has made some reforms and investments in its economy, but the world recession has blunted much progress. Kyrgyzstan, Tajikistan, and Uzbekistan are poor nations still struggling for national purpose after dissolution of the Soviet Empire. Poor agriculture based on irrigation, semi-nomadic herding, oil in Uzbekistan, and attractive mountainous desert environments are about the only resources of these isolated and landlocked nations. Their proximity to Afghanistan, Pakistan, China, and Iran give them some strategic importance. The United Nations and United States' operations in Afghanistan have stimulated some economic activity here. Uzbekistan's 28 million people are particularly disadvantaged by their being trafficked around for forced labor in Russia, and girls and women forced into the sexual slavery trade to surrounding nations and Asia.

Table 9.2
Percentage of Population Below the Poverty Line

Rank	Country	% Below	Rank	Country	% Below
1	Finland	1	133	Honduras	59
2	Taiwan	1	134	Bolivia	60
3	Kuwait	2	135	Congo Rep	60
4	China	3	136	Rwanda	60
5	Ireland	4	137	Tajikistan	60
6	Lithuania	4	138	Niger	63
7	Norway	4	139	N. Korea	66
8	Tunisia	4	140	Burundi	68
9	Japan	5	141	Zimbabwe	68
10	Malaysia	5	142	Swaziland	69
11	Singapore	5	143	Congo Zaire	70
12	Australia	6	144	Mozambique	70

Rank	Country	% Below	Rank	Country	% Below
13	Austria	6	145	Nigeria	70
14	Czech Rep	6	146	Sierra Leone	70
15	France	6	147	Chad	80
16	Italy	6	148	Haiti	80
17	New Zealand	6	149	Liberia	80
18	Sweden	6	150	Somalia	80
36	U.S.A.	12	151	Zambia	86

Source: CIA World Factbook, 2011.

Note: Each country defines its own "Poverty Level"; distortions in the Table above are evident

Table 9.3
World Patents Granted, 2006

Rank	Country	Number Granted	% World Total	GDP/C
1	Japan	217,364	32	$32,600
2	U.S.A.	154,760	23	46,400
3	S. Korea	102,633	15	28,000
4	Germany	56,091	8	34,100
5	China	26,292	4	6,600
6	France	25,683	4	32,800
7	Russia	19,641	3	15,100
8	U.K.	13,183	2	35,200
9	Netherlands	9,949	1	39,200
10	Switzerland	9,857	1	41,700
11	Canada	8,188	1	38,400
12	Sweden	7,224	1	36,800
13	Finland	4,341	.6	34,900
14	Australia	4,163	.6	38,800
15	Austria	3,537	.5	39,400
16	Spain	3,221	.5	33,700
17	Ukraine	2,889	.3	6,400
18	Belgium	2,773	.3	36,600
19	Israel	2,534	.3	28,400
20	India	2,267	.3	3,100
21	Poland	1,216	.1	17,900
22	Norway	1,138	.1	56,600
23	Belarus	1,120	.1	11,600

Source: United Nations World Intellectual Property Organization

Infrastructure to support primary, secondary, and tertiary industries is indispensable to promote a program of economic development. Infrastructure includes a transportation system, a telecommunications system, a power grid system, a waste management system, a water supply system, a warehousing-distribution system, a marketing system, a financial investment system, an international trading system, a labor market, a raw materials and component parts system, a research and development system, and a legal system that protects patents and facilitates business organizations. A proactive government structure is essential for the more costly infrastructure facilities, while private businesses can build others. Sometimes governments build large "industrial parks" which feature already installed infrastructure and even buildings that enhance and enable the benefits of "agglomeration economies," or the benefit of close physical association of many linked businesses.

Of course, sometimes governments run business operations themselves. China's military runs a good deal of that nation's electronics industry. The collapse of Soviet style "command economies" is ample proof that governments do a poor job of operating industries for economic production. In the United States, consider the inefficient operations and consistent monetary losses of the Post Office Department. The "laissez faire" business model which periodically expels inefficient users of resources by forcing them out of business, while efficient users of resources prosper has proven most efficient in the long run.

Rich countries have extensive infrastructure facilities, formed over many years. This gives entrepreneurs a rich environment for founding new businesses. Poor countries need to develop at least rudimentary infrastructure to stimulate economic growth, but investment in infrastructure does not automatically insure the development of new businesses, so investment in infrastructure incurs risks that poor governments are reluctant to take.

Table 9.2 lists the nations with the highest and lowest percentages of their populations below the "poverty line." The fact that each nation defines its own poverty line must be recognized when interpreting the information from this table. For instance, to think that China and Tunisia have only 2 and 3 percent of their populations below the poverty line is not realistic. China probably has at least 50% of its population in the poor category, based on its 57% rural residents, and Tunisia has 50% of its population poor, based on a 15% unemployment rate, its low GDP/Capita of $8,000, and its uneven family income distribution. All the other nations from 1 through 18 have actively improving economies with no laggard sections. Even agriculture is a productive enterprise for their rural citizens. In fact, China's large rural population has been left behind during the recent economic spurt and experts believe that this may prove a serious problem in the future.

Nations from 133 to 151 are the poorest of the world's poor nations. Haiti, Bolivia, Honduras, and North Korea have experienced little or no growth over the past 50 years. Population growth in excess of economic growth creates a growing poverty-stricken class which threatens to become a "vicious circle of poverty." Tajikistan and the African countries have similar experiences. Low investment, declining infrastructure, and growing populations doom these nations to what only can be called increasing human misery.

Table 9.3 lists the number of patents issued in various nations in 2006, the latest date for which data are available. Seventy eight % of the patents in 2006 were granted to residents of just 4 nations, Japan, U.S.A., South Korea, and Germany. This is a good indicator of the dynamism of these national economies and the entrepreneurial skills of their inhabitants. This economic dynamism presages future growth of their productivity. China, Ukraine, Belarus, India, and Poland are relative newcomers in the entrepreneurial elite nations. Their substantial contribution to increased productivity predict a future of better economic growth than they have experienced in the past. Globalization, of course, means that technology transfers from one nation to another, in the form of licensing, branch plants of innovators, outright gifts, and technology sales can help adopting nations to share in the world's growing prosperity. As the rich and semi-rich nations continue to develop economically, hopefully, some of this economic human well-being will make lives in the world's poor nations less burdensome.

ENDNOTES

1. Kissinger, Henry, *Diplomacy*, New York: Simon and Schuster, 1994.

2, Friedman, Thomas L., *Hot, Flat, And Crowded: Why We Need A Green Revolution—And How It Can Renew America*, New York: Farrar, Straus, and Giroux, 2008, p. 147.

3. CIA, World Factbook 2011, New York: Skyhorse Publishing, 2010.

Chapter Ten
World Political Systems, Status and Trends

A nation's Political System has the overall responsibility for seeking human well-being for its citizens. Specific jobs of government are: 1. Provide domestic and international order; 2. Provide freedom for responsible individuals and groups to attain all levels of Maslow's hierarchy of human needs[1] 3. Provide justice in arbitrating disputes among citizens and citizen groups; 4. Provide government legitimacy by holding frequent and fair elections. Governments must make and enforce laws that insure the efficient and productive operations of all four national systems, to aid them in attaining human well-being for their people's present and future needs.

Balancing apparently conflicting interests is one of government's most difficult tasks. Balancing the productive use of natural resources while preserving the goal of environmental preservation; balancing social cohesion versus protecting individual and group rights; balancing economic efficiency and business incentives versus income egalitarianism; balancing order and freedom are all examples of tasks which governments must constantly monitor to correct any problems that arise to threaten human well-being. Political Systems must extract resources from their citizens and spend resources to operate the agencies that are supposed to promote human well-being in all its forms. Legitimacy is the citizens' feeling and action that their government is carrying out its obligations to help citizens attain the highest social, economic, and political goals.

> The system of free markets and liberal democracy that now characterizes most of the developed world may be flawed; it may all too often reflect the interests of the powerful over the powerless. But that system is constantly subject to change and improvement—and it is precisely this openness to change that market-based liberal democracies offer people around the world their best chance at a better life.[2]

Unfortunately, there is no simple set of statistics that can capture the full extent of good government operations as opposed to bad government operations. Government support of education was considered and rejected; government support of health care was considered and rejected; government expenditures of infrastructure investment was considered and rejected; media freedom and availability was considered and rejected. Fortunately, Freedom House, a U.S.A based NGO rates nations each year on civil liberties, political rights, and overall citizen freedoms. Existence of a competitive multi-party political system, universality of adult voting rights, voting fairness, and access of political parties to the electorate are some of the most important criteria behind the Freedom House rankings. A nation earns a score of 1 for highest civil liberties and a 7 for worst civil liberties; and the same accounting is used for political rights. An overall rating of 2 to 5, and the country earns a label of "free"; a rating of 6 to 10 earns a rating of "partly free"; and a rating of 11 to 14 earns a rating of "not free." Because there is a limited range of numbers—2 to 14—many nations receive the same rating scores. Such nations in Table 10.1 are listed alphabetically in their categories, and their political score is the average ranking for their freedom—non-freedom status when we attempt to measure the degree of political human well-being in each nation.

The complete data for the Political System are shown on Table Ap.4 in the Statistical Appendix and on Table 10.1 below. Table Ap.4 shows that 28 of the world's 151 nations rank as "free," almost twice as many as were rated "free" in 1972, the first date for which data are available. Chile recovered from the Pinochet dictatorship, and the demise of the Soviet Union freed the Czech Republic, Estonia, Hungary, Lithuania, Poland, Slovakia, Slovenia from the Soviet yoke, and Uruguay was lifted from "partly free" to a status of perfect political freedom. Table 10.1 confirms this conclusion and adds Bosnia and Herzegovina, Moldova, Mozambique, Papua New Guinea, Timor L'Este, Georgia, Guinea-Bissau, Burundi, Uganda, Armenia, and Central African Republic to the list of "partly free" nations. Gain of some civil and political liberties in Africa is particularly noteworthy.

Table Ap.4 lists some 43 of the world's nations as "not free," with most of these nations from Africa and the Middle East. Eritrea, Libya, Myanmar, North Korea, Somalia, Sudan, Turkmenistan, and Uzbekistan share the ignominy of being rated as the world's most oppressive regimes. Belarus, Chad, China, Cuba, Guinea, Laos, Saudi Arabia, and Syria are virtually indistinguishable from this latter group. While political liberalism has made good worldwide gains—the world average indicating a "partly free world"—perhaps the beacon of newly liberalized regimes will convince the laggards that they should make serious attempts to improve their citizens' human well-being from the Political System.

Table 10.1
Largest Gains in Civil and Political Liberties, 1972-2010

(Worst in Freedoms = 14; Best in Freedoms = 2)*

Rank	Country	Gain	1972	2010
1	Czech Rep	12	14	2
2	Estonia	12	14	2
3	Lithuania	12	14	2
4	Slovakia	12	14	2
5	Slovenia	12	14	2
6	Croatia	11	14	3
7	Bulgaria	10	14	4
8	Latvia	10	14	4
9	Mongolia	10	14	4
10	Serbia	10	14	4
11	Albania	9	14	5
12	Macedonia	8	14	6
13	Moldova	8	14	6
14	Bosnia & Herz	7	14	7
15	Georgia	7	14	7
16	Mozambique	7	14	7
17	Papua N G	7	14	7
18	Timor L'Este	7	14	7
19	Ukraine	7	14	7
20	Guinea-Bissau	6	14	8
21	Uganda	5	14	9
22	Armenia	4	14	10
23	Burundi	4	14	10
24	Cent Af Rep	4	14	10
25	Kyrgyzstan	4	14	10
26	Azerbaijan	3	14	11
27	Iraq	3	14	11
28	Kazakhstan	3	14	11
29	Russia	3	14	11
30	Tajikistan	3	14	11
31	Yemen	3	14	11

1972 World Mean = 10 2010 World Mean = 7
** Ratings by freedom house.org; See: Table Ap.4, Statistical Appendix*

Table 10.2 lists the "Failed States" Index, based on a dozen social, economic, and political factors. Nearly one-third of the world's 151 nations are on this list, a shameful condemnation of these nations and the United Nations efforts to bring peace and prosperity to the world's nations during more than 60 years of efforts to do so. Without an effective government, improvement in the human condition is impossible. Somalia and Eritrea have the rule of bands of marauding thugs, while Afghanistan and Iraq suffer the disorganization of civil war. Myanmar, North Korea, Syria, Congo Zaire, and Cambodia have the rule of self-serving dictators. Zimbabwe, Kenya, Uganda, Malawi, Lebanon, Colombia, and Egypt all have favorable resource bases, relatively homogeneous societies, and some former progress in human well-being. Something dramatic needs to happen to get these and other nations on that list to get on the path toward economic-social-political development. Maybe regional organizations such as the European Union can overcome past failures to bring these nations into the modern world. The United Nations must lead the way; surely it now has enough experience in its development agenda to surmount past inertia and take a more active and effective role in promoting more efforts at securing a program of true betterment of human well-being.

> Looking at dozens of countries over decades of development, from South Korea to Argentina to Turkey, one finds that the pattern is strong—a market-based economy that achieves middle income status tends over the long run, toward liberal democracy. It may be, as many scholars have noted, the single most important and well-documented generalization in Political Science.[3]

Table 10.2
The Failed States Index

Rank	Country	Index	Rank	Country	Index
1	Somalia	114.7	25	Cameroon	95.3
2	Zimbabwe	114	26	Guinea-Bissau	94.8
3	Sudan	112.4	27	Malawi	93.8
4	Congo Zaire	108.7	28	Lebanon	93.5
5	Iraq	108.6	29	Congo Rep	92.1
6	Afghanistan	108.2	30	Uzbekistan	92.8
7	Cent Af Rep	105.4	31	Sierra Leone	92.8
8	Guinea	104.6	32	Georgia	91.8
9	Pakistan	104.1	33	Liberia	91.8
10	Cote D'Ivoire	102.5	34	Burkina Faso	91.3
11	Haiti	101.8	35	Eritrea	90.3
12	Myanmar	101.5	36	Tajikistan	90.3
13	Kenya	101.4	37	Iran	90.0
14	Nigeria	99.8	38	Syria	89.8
15	Ethiopia	98.9	39	Colombia	89.2
16	North Korea	98.3	40	Kyrgyzstan	89.1
17	Yemen	98.1	41	Egypt	89.0
18	Bangladesh	98.1	42	Laos	89.0

Rank	Country	Index	Rank	Country	Index
19	Timor L'Este	97.2	43	Rwanda	89.0
20	Uganda	96.9	44	Mauritania	88.7
21	Sri Lanka	96.7	45	Cambodia	87.3
22	Niger	96.5	46	Togo	87.2
23	Burundi	95.7	47	Bolivia	86.3
24	Nepal	95.4			

Source: Fundforpeace.org; Index is based on 12 social, economic, and political factors.

ENDNOTES

1. Maslow, Abraham, *Motivation and Personality*, New York: Harper and Row, 1954

2. Obama, Barak, *The Audacity Of Hope: Thoughts On Reclaiming The American Dream*, New York: Crown Publishers, 2006, p. 316.

3. Zakaria, Fareed, *The Post American World*, New York and London: W.H. Norton and Company, 2008, p. 102

Chapter Eleven

World Human Well-Being, Status and Trends

At the beginning of this book, we built a model that stated that a nation's human well-being is derived from its Physical System, Social System, Economic System, and its Political System. Now we need a method to combine all four systems to get an overall measure of human well-being as it varies among the world's 151 nations included in this book. Complicating the matter, we have two money indicators (PPP), one rate indicator, and one judgment indicator with a limited range of numbers. One simple way to reconcile these differences is to add the world rank of a nation on each of the four systems. The nation with the best possible total rankings (we interpret this as highest human well-being) would be 1 for the Physical System, 1 for the Social System, 1 for the Economic System, and 14 for the Political System (34 nations have the highest rank, a perfect score of 2 on political freedom; therefore all these nations are assigned the average ranking of 14). Thus our best possible score for human well-being would be 1, plus 1, plus 1, plus 14 or a score of 17 for all four systems combined. These ranks can be extracted from Tables Ap.1, Ap.2, Ap.3, Ap.4 in the Statistical Appendix.

Let's look at the scores for the United States rankings in 2010 to illustrate this method. From Table Ap.1 in 2010, the U.S.A. ranked 83rd in the world in Agriculture Value Added per capita (PPP); Table Ap.2 ranks the nation 28th in the world in Infant Mortality rates; Table Ap.3 ranks the U.S.A. 4th in the world in GDP/Capita (PPP) in 2010; Table Ap.4 ranks the U.S.A. 14th in the world (average rank for 27 nations with the same perfect civil and political liberties scores). Total combined world rankings for the U.S.A. are: 83 plus 28, plus 4, plus 14 = 129. A "Four Systems Cumulative World Ranking of 129 places the U.S.A. 22nd in the world in our measure of "human well-being." How could the U.S.A. rank so low, not even in the world's top 10% of nations? Clearly these numbers tell us that 83rd rank in what we have interpreted as the productivity of the Physical System is the chief cause of this low ranking, but 28th ranking in the Social System is another important factor in depressing the overall score.

> The mutually supportive combination of public and private development; the excellence of the universities; the unmatched ability to attract and absorb the world's talent—these are assets we can work to preserve.[1]

As we noted in Chapter 6 on the Physical System, rich nations have tended to neglect investment in the agricultural sector, favoring investment to secondary and tertiary industries. This leaves a lot of the world's primary industries to the poor nations. We even noted that several domestic programs in the U.S.A. have paid farmers not to produce agricultural goods. The higher rate of infant mortality among the world's rich nations seems indeed to signal a serious dysfunction in its Social System. Having more than 37 million people below the poverty line is a social ill with many causes. If the U.S. government wishes to improve human well-being of all its citizens, it needs to address these issues and to seek remedies.

Eleven of the top nations in the world in human well-being are part of the European Union (SEE: Table Ap.5 in the Statistical Appendix); the other four are closely related to the Western Nations. Table 11.1 shows that six of the highest gainers in human well-being are nations which joined the European Union since 1973. Note that all changes on this table are negative numbers which indicates that the nation ranked higher in 2010 than it did in 1960. In order to join the European Union, candidate nations must fulfill basic economic and political conditions, including a free market and democratic political institutions. Portugal, Spain, Greece, Finland, Ireland, and many nations of the former Soviet Satellites of Eastern Europe have made tremendous improvements in human well-being during the past three decades. Perhaps this model of economic-social-political development should be studied by the United Nations. Then the United Nations could devise a program of multiple nation organizations which would receive aid as a whole if they made economic-social-political reforms. Stressing ECONOMIC DEVELOPMENT has not worked particularly well in the past.

Table 11.2 lists the nations that suffered the worst declines in human well-being from 1960 to 2010. Again note that the changes for each nation are expressed in positive numbers, which indicates their lower ranking in the world on the sum of all four systems; thus lower human well-being. Ten of the fifteen nations, designated with an (F), are on Table 10.2, "Failed States Index." For whatever reason, ineffective governments doom a nation to low levels of human well-being. Indeed, 26 of the world's 30 nations with the lowest human well-being are considered failed states. (See: Table Ap.5, Statistical Appendix). What possible hope do these nations have for raising human well-being? Even massive humanitarian aid brings only a little relief. Somehow, effective political systems must emerge. While it may only be a pipedream, what the world really needs is a complete redrawing of the political national boundary lines. It might take on the form of the European Union, a strong central core of one or more nations demanding political and economic reform of members who wish to join. Combined physical resources of the new nation might be a draw to join. Some ineffective attempts to create regional organizations have failed in the past. LAFTA, CAFTA, CARICOM, ASEAN, NAFTA, and a host of other alphabet soup attempts probably soured planners on this approach. Why cannot the

United Nations lead in making such organizations the basis of all new development projects?

Table 11.1
Greatest Gains in Human Well-Being, 1960-2010 in Terms of World Rankings

	Country		Ag VA	Inf Mort	GDP/C	Freedom	Total
1	China	1960	138	107	138	129	512
		2010	47	66	76	140	329
2	Chile	1960	86	76	45	88	295
		2010	49	37	40	14	140
3	Slovakia #	1960	81	19	23	129	252
		2010	20	33	32	14	99
4	Macedonia	1960	58	78	69	129	334
		2010	19	41	67	64	191
5	Serbia	1960	69	59	29	129	286
		2010	7	33	61	45	146
6	Czech Rep #	1960	85	7	16	129	237
		2010	51	10	29	14	104
7	S. Korea	1960	40	61	104	24	229
		2010	31	10	23	33	97
8	Bosnia &	1960	96	69	94	129	388
	Herz	2010	64	41	81	75	261
9	Lithuania #	1960	47	36	57	129	269
		2010	56	33	39	14	142
10	Spain #	1960	28	29	46	71	174
		2010	14	10	25	14	63
11	Bulgaria #	1960	67	32	63	129	291
		2010	23	61	52	45	181
12	Albania	1960	33	71	83	129	316
		2010	8	64	73	64	209
13	Thailand	1960	121	68	120	47	356
		2010	22	61	70	98	251
14	Poland #	1960	55	43	38	88	224
		2010	37	33	36	14	120
15	Mali	1960	125	151	143	102	521
		2010	89	147	131	55	422
106	U.S.A.	1960	46	11	3	8	68
		2010	83	28	4	14	129

Sources: Tables Ap.1, Ap.2, Ap.3, Ap.4, Statistical Appendix

 # = Member of the European Union

Table 11.2
Worst Declines in Human Well-Being, 1960-2010

	Country		Ag Va	Inf Mort	GDP/C	Freedom	Total
151	Zimbabwe	1960	99	65	142	71	377
	(F)	2010	151	92	151	131	525
150	Lebanon (F)	1960	18	45	34	24	121
		2010	60	72	45	87	264
149	Iraq(F)	1960	79	74	21	129	303
		2010	125	100	96	118	439
148	Jamaica	1960	63	38	39	17	157
		2010	107	53	72	55	287
147	Nicaragua	1960	38	90	68	47	243
		2010	100	80	102	87	369
146	Somalia (F)	1960	72	150	108	102	432
		2010	116	146	147	148	557
145	N. Korea (F)	1960	72	57	98	129	356
		2010	110	107	115	148	480
144	Cameroon (F)	1960	74	110	106	57	347
		2010	109	120	109	131	469
143	Afghanistan	1960	72	148	124	102	446
	(F)	2010	138	150	142	131	561
142	Zambia	1960	122	83	102	57	364
		2010	133	144	124	75	476
141	Switzerland	1960	4	7	2	8	21
		2010	99	10	5	14	128
140	Gabon	1960	7	82	33	88	210
		2010	41	109	43	118	311
139	Mauritania	1960	52	128	119	88	387
	(F)	2010	137	120	112	118	487
138	Niger (F)	1960	102	143	122	57	424
		2010	134	148	144	98	524
137	Kenya (F)	1960	100	79	121	47	347
		2010	126	112	121	87	446

Sources: Tables Ap.1, Ap.2, Ap.3, Ap.4, Statistical Appendix
(F) = Listed On Table 10-2, "Failed States Index"

ENDNOTES

1. SEE: Fallows, James, "How America Can Rise Again," *The Atlantic*, January-February 2010, pp. 54-61.

Chapter Twelve

Comparison of the Four Systems Index with Other Measures of Human Development

Many other measures of human development have been proposed; does our "Four Systems Index" offer any insights into the modernization of the world's nations that other measures do not? That is the question we will explore in this chapter. Probably the best known other measure is the United Nations Human Development Programme's Human Development Index "HDI."

> The cover of the 2010 Human Development report illustrates the complex multiple pathways of Human Development over the four decades documented in this 20th Anniversary edition. Each single strand depicts one country's Human Development Index over time.
>
> The overall global pattern is one of remarkable human progress: people around the world are, on average, living longer, with greater access to knowledge and with higher incomes. Yet progress is rarely constant or linear. For some countries one or more of the underlying indicators has changed little or even declined over the period. The greatest relative advance has been experienced by people in countries on the lower end of the human development scale, achievements often attained despite conflicts, epidemics, economic setbacks and other adversities.
>
> Analysis of the annual Human Development Index and three new complimentary indexes introduced in the 2010 Report provides new insights into these trends and offers important lessons for the future.[1]

The Human Development Index (HDI) considers only three variables: Longevity, Education, and Gross National Income. According to the Human Well-Being Index developed in this book, human well-being comes from all four of a nation's macro systems: Physical System, Social System, Economic System, and Political System. Because the United Nations Development Programme's (UNDP) Index only includes indicators from the social and economic systems, it is clear that this index fails to say anything about two vital components of the concept of "Human Well-Being," Freedom, and the Physical Environment. The U N itself suffers the blindness created by its need for "political correctness." For instance, it ignores Taiwan completely in deference to China's wishes. Taiwan is one of the greatest success stories in improving human well-being in the world over the past 50 years. Certainly the U N misses the mark on "...providing insights..." about human development by ignoring Taiwan.

The UNDP quote above also claims that the greatest improvement in human development has been experienced by people from nations at the lower end of the human development scale. Certainly this is not true when we include civil and political freedoms into our concept of human well-being. From Table Ap-5 in the Statistical Appendix, our measure of the Four Systems Index shows that Finland, Spain, Austria, Greece, Slovakia, Czech Republic, Croatia, Poland, Slovenia, Lithuania, Serbia, Hungary, Estonia, Bulgaria, Romania, Macedonia, and Latvia, mostly middle developed nations in 1960, have risen to new heights of human well-being by 2010. Freedom from the yoke of "Central Planning," and major economic, legal, and political reforms required by association with the European Union were vital factors in this astounding increase in human well-being. If the UNDP truly seeks "...new insights into these trends...," it would do well to study these cases carefully and thoroughly.

An analysis of the trends in human well-being also provides strong evidence of the efficacy of our "Four Systems Index" over that offered by the HDI. Table 12.1 compares the Four Systems ranking of the top 10% of nations experiencing the greatest and those that experienced the least gains in human well-being compared to those identified by the HDI. In both the greatest gains and the least gains, there are agreements in rankings on only three nations in the greatest gains category and three in the least gains category. South Korea, Serbia, and Indonesia are on both lists of gains, while only Afghanistan, Iraq, and Zimbabwe are on both lists of declining human well-being. War-torn Afghanistan and Iraq are obvious candidates on any list of human deprivation; people of these nations have sunk below Maslow's second level of "Safety and Security" in his hierarchy of human needs.[2]

The Four Systems Index was specifically designed to trace changes over time, the HDI was not, although discussions in their annual reports imply the UNDP is vitally concerned with change over time. Therefore, comparisons of change recorded by the two indices should be made with caution.

Table 12.1
Biggest Gains in Human Well-Being, HDI VS 4 Systems

Country	HDI	World Rank	Country	4 Systems
Taiwan	190	1	China	-151
Egypt	186	2	Chile	-133
Algeria	166	3	S. Korea	-128
S. Korea	164	4	Slovakia	-120
Tunisia	164	5	Ireland	-116
Serbia	160	6	Bosnia & Herz	-108
Saudi Arabia	141	7	Macedonia	-108
China	133	8	Serbia	-108
Malaysia	133	9	Thailand	-107

Country	HDI	World Rank	Country	4 Systems
Morocco	132	10	Sierra Leone	-103
Iran	131	11	Czech Rep	-101
Indonesia	129	12	Spain	-96
Nepal	127	13	Lithuania	-92
Bolivia	124	14	Indonesia	-86
Botswana	124	15	Croatia	-82
U.S.A.	66	104		
Eritrea	-31	137	Cuba	118
Haiti	-38	138	Mauritania	124
S. Africa	-53	139	Afghanistan	129
Zambia	-54	140	Gabon	129
Afghanistan	-57	141	Cameroon	133
Guinea	-66	142	Nicaragua	134
Lesotho	-72	143	Jamaica	138
Ethiopia	-78	144	Venezuela	140
Sierra Leone	-89	145	Lebanon	147
Russia	-96	146	Zimbabwe	159
Liberia	-106	147	Madagascar	162
Mozambique	-122	148	Kuwait	163
Iraq	-126	149	Swaziland	163
Congo Zaire	-176	150	Iraq	170
Zimbabwe	-410	151	North Korea	198

Source: Tables Ap.5 and Ap.6, Statistical Appendix.

Nevertheless, the list of Egypt, Algeria, Tunisia, Saudi Arabia, Morocco, Iran, Nepal, and Bolivia in the top 10% of world nations in human development over the past 35 years (the first HDI was published in 1975) is surreal. All these nations suffer from political repression, social backwardness, and mostly economic imbalances. Taiwan, a true success story in the improvement in the human condition, is on the list only because of our estimated values; the UNDP ignores this progressive nation. On the other end of the scale of human well-being, the UNDP ignores the economic and political disruptions of Communist Cuba and North Korea, the mismanagement of resources and turmoil in Jamaica, Nicaragua, and Venezuela, Lebanon's quasi colonial status, and the low development levels of Mauritania, Cameroon, Madagascar, and Swaziland.

Table 12.1 provides clear evidence that the Four Systems Index offers more profound, definitive, and realistic evaluations of the development status than does the UNDP's HDI Index. *Newsweek* magazine rated 100 of the world's nations in a special August 2010 article entitled: "The Best Countries in the World."[3] Foroohar ranks countries on Education, Health, Quality of Life, Economic Dynamism, and Political Environment dimensions. An erudite panel of experts aided in the selection of data, weighting of variables, and in making cross-nation comparisons. These variables are run through a weighted formula and each nation is awarded a score of from 0 to 100 and arranged in numerical order. Only 100 nations were rated in this fashion, out of a total of 151 nations in our universe. Therefore we will confine our comparison of *Newsweek*'s and the 4 Systems Index of only the top ranking 30 nations (20% of our data set). The lowest rankings would be distorted by the different sample size.

> Foroohar posed the following question:
>
> If you were born today, which country would provide you with the very best opportunity to live a healthy, safe, reasonably prosperous, and upwardly mobile life? [4]

The author concludes that a "...good, broad based educational system is crucial—it's very clearly linked to future economic prosperity..." Long term peace and economic dynamism then lead to a healthy and high quality of life. Table 12.2 compares the *Newsweek* 30 best countries with our 4 Systems Index of best 30 countries. The two lists are highly correlated. Singapore is the major difference, ranking 19th on the *Newsweek* list and 54th on the 4 Systems List (See: Table Ap.5 in the Statistical Appendix). Limited physical resources, especially space—after all, this "nation" is little more than a city state – and restrictions on personal civil and political freedoms depress human well-being according to our evaluation. *Newsweek* also rates Germany, Japan, U.K., Switzerland, and Belgium relatively higher than the 4 Systems Index does. Four Systems ranks Slovakia, Spain, Greece, Ireland, Croatia, and the Czech Republic slightly higher than *Newsweek* does. The latter nations have made large gains during the past 50 years in all aspects of human well-being, largely explained by the association with the European Union and its demands for reforms.

Table 12.2
Newsweek*'s Best Countries VS 4 Systems Index Best Countries*

Country	Happiness	World Rank	Country	4 Systems
Finland	89	1	Norway	35
Switzerland	89	2	Denmark	40
Sweden	89	3	Australia	45
Australia	87	4	Ireland	49
Norway	87	5	Finland	53
Canada	87	6	Spain	63
Netherlands	86	7	New Zealand	73
Japan	85	8	Netherlands	87
Denmark	85	9	Austria	91
U.S.A.	85	10	France	92
Germany	84	11	Greece	94
New Zealand	84	12	S. Korea	97
U.K.	83	13	Slovakia	99
S. Korea	83	14	Czech Rep	104

Country	Happiness	World Rank	Country	4 Systems
France	83	15	Sweden	104
Ireland	83	16	Croatia	109
Austria	82	17	Israel	114
Belgium	82	18	Canada	116
Singapore	80	19	Uruguay	119
Spain	80	20	Poland	120
Israel	79	21	Switzerland	128
Italy	78	22	U.S.A.	129
Slovenia	78	23	Slovenia	132
Czech Rep	77	24	Portugal	134
Greece	76	25	Chile	140
Portugal	76	26	Lithuania	142
Croatia	74	27	Serbia	146
Poland	74	28	Italy	149
Chile	74	29	Hungary	155
Slovakia	73	30	Japan	159

Sources: Tables Ap.5 and Ap.7, Statistical Appendix

Thus we can say that the status of the world's nations in human well-being is successfully described about equally well by *Newsweek*'s list and the 4 Systems Index list. You could choose a country to prosper in from either list, personal proclivities as your final guide to your new residence. Our list of nations to avoid is more comprehensive. The 4 Systems Index adds a second dimension, however, the trend over the past 50 years. *Newsweek* did not address this issue directly, although their "Economic Dynamism" factor hints at it.

Ruut Veenhoven at Erasmus University of Rotterdam is the head of an institute which keeps a "World Database of Happiness," described as a "continuous register of scientific research on subjective appreciation of life."[5] Now we must understand that "happiness" is a state of mind, not necessarily the same thing as human well-being as we have defined that term. Apparently, Veenhoven's researchers question people in various countries about their feelings of happiness. The results are then fed into the above cited database. In spite of the differences in concepts, it might be worthwhile to compare the 4 Systems Index of nations with Veenhoven's list of nation's feelings of "happiness." A look at Table 12.3 gives us the results. Only 16 nations considered to have high human well-being by the 4 Systems Index are on the list of nations whose citizens are happy. On the latter list, Costa Rica—number one in the world of happiness -, Mexico, Panama, Colombia, Dominican Republic, and Brazil all are considered in the happiest category. There seems to be a Latin American bias in the Happiness Index. In the least happy category, only Burundi and Mozambique make both lists. Most of the unhappy countries are poor African countries, plus Haiti, Timor L'Este, and Turkmenistan.

Without more information about the questions asked of people in these surveys on subjective appreciation of life, all we can conclude is that it seems that happiness and human well-being are slightly different concepts. Maybe Psychologists can study these issues and shed some more light on the world's human development problems.

Table 12.3
Comparison of Happiness VS 4 Systems Indices

Country	Happiness	World Rank	Country	4 Systems
Costa Rica	8.5	1	Norway	35
Denmark	8.3	2	Denmark	40
Switzerland	8.0	3	Australia	45
Finland	7.9	4	Ireland	49
Mexico	7.9	5	Finland	53
Norway	7.9	6	Spain	63
Canada	7.8	7	New Zealand	73
Panama	7.8	8	Netherlands	87
Sweden	7.8	9	Austria	91
Australia	7.7	10	France	92
Austria	7.7	11	Greece	94
Colombia	7.7	12	S. Korea	97
Dominican Rep	7.6	13	Slovakia	99
Ireland	7.6	14	Czech Rep	104
Netherlands	7.6	15	Sweden	104
Brazil	7.5	16	Croatia	109
U.S.A. ranks 18th, "Above Average" Happiness				
Timor L'Este	4.0	137	Liberia	490
Turkmenistan	4.0	138	Myanmar	491
Cameroon	3.8	139	Ethiopia	494
Haiti	3.9	140	Guinea-Bissau	498
Mozambique	3.8	141	Mozambique	500
Niger	3.8	142	Rwanda	501
Congo Zaire	3.7	143	Cent Af Rep	502
Kenya	3.7	144	Burundi	520
Madagascar	3.7	145	Niger	524
Sierra Leone	3.0	146	Zimbabwe	525
Benin	3.0	147	Eritrea	536
Zimbabwe	3.0	148	Guinea	542
Burundi	2.9	149	Somalia	557
Tanzania	2.8	150	Afghanistan	561
Togo	2.6	151	Congo Zaire	561

Sources: Tables Ap.5 and Ap.7, Statistical Appendix

ENDNOTES

1. See: United Nations, U N Development Programme, *Human Development Report 2010*, Oxford: Oxford University Press, 2010, p. 2

2. See: Maslow, Abraham, *Motivation And Personality*, New York: Harper and Row, 1954.

3. Foroohar, Rana, "The Best Countries in the World," *Newsweek*, August 23, and 30, 2010, pp. 30-42.

4. See: Foroohar, Rana, Ibid.

5. Veenhoven, Ruut, World Database of Happiness, Erasmus University, Rotterdam, Holland.

Chapter Thirteen
Conclusions: Human Well-Being around the World

In the foregoing pages we have developed an index of human well-being that clearly differentiates the world's nations based on quantitative empirical data. Human well-being comes from a nation's Physical, Social, Economic, and Political Systems. There are numerous and complex interrelationships among all four systems which enhance human well-being or detract from it. The world's development planners should consider the improvement of all four systems when devising programs of "economic development."

Maybe improvements in the economy must come first—that is the traditional model most of the rich nations of the world today have followed. Fidel Castro tried a social revolution first and the results have not raised Cuba to a new level of human well-being during the past 50 years. In fact, that nation has actually regressed in human well-being over that time period. Kemal Attaturk tried a revolution from the top down, a somewhat novel approach. That one succeeded quickly in the urban areas of Turkey, but progress was much slower in the rural areas. Attaturk's reforms were based on copying the institutions of Western Europe. After about 80 years of tumultuous international affairs, Turkey has recently applied for membership in the European Union. Their admission—still pending—would bring Turkey full circle from a decadent Middle East past into a modern liberal democratic future.

The Russian/Chinese model of "central planning," recently modified by "free market" institutions, has displayed good growth potential during the past decade. Surely there are numerous models of development that might be tried, each one geared to the circumstances of individual nations; the Japan-Taiwan-South Korea models of growth have brought huge increases in human well-being to those fortunate nations.

Examination of the world ranking of nations by the 4 Systems Index with other indices of "development" shows broad agreement among all these indices. The 4 Systems Index approach seems to offer the best and most comprehensive measurement of progress in human well-being. Our results have revealed the status AND trends in human development which other indices we examined did not do. Statistical results of our analysis pointed to "problem areas" in national development even of the richest nations, whether they be in physical, social, economic, or political realms. This type of analysis should prove beneficial in all nations, whether rich or poor, in planning future development projects.

According to the 4 Systems model, the following nations have increased their overall human well-being rankings most with respect to the rest of the world: China (56), Mongolia (47), Chile (46), Bosnia & Herzegovina (44), Macedonia (44), Timor L'Este (43), Thailand (40), Indonesia (38), Slovakia (38), Serbia (37), Mali (36), Albania (34), Tunisia (34), Lithuania (33), Albania (30), and Ghana (30). The following countries have slipped the most: Venezuela (55), Madagascar (52), Nicaragua (52), Swaziland (50), Kuwait (44), Tajikistan (42), Iraq (41), Jamaica (41), Gabon (40), Lebanon (40), Zimbabwe (39), Cameroon (38), Cuba (38), and North Korea (36). Studying all these nations for positive and negative features of their past activities should point the way to more positive development planning.

Simple models are much prized over more complex ones. Some have suggested that GDP/Capita alone can tell us all we need to know about human well-being. There is no question that wealth makes a major contribution to all other aspects of human well-being, but that wealth must be spent wisely to improve the lives of people in any nation. Great wealth in Saudi Arabia, Kuwait, U.A.E., Iraq, and Nigeria has not brought universal human well-being to their citizens. Oil wealth of Norway, on the other hand, has catapulted that nation to the top of all lists of human well-being.

Table 13.1 compares a ranking of nations in GDP/Capita (PPP) with our 4 Systems Index. Approximately half of the rankings of the richest nations and poorest nations coincide with our ranking of human well-being. Singapore tops the list of GDP/Capita but only ranks 54th on the 4 Systems Index for reasons stated above. Kuwait and U.A.E. rank highly on the GDP/Capita list but only 62nd and 64th on the 4 Systems list. Finland, Spain, New Zealand, France, Greece, South Korea, Slovakia, and Czech Republic all are on the 4 Systems list of top 10% of the world's nations in human well-being, but they fail to make the top 10% of the GDP/Capita list.

Poverty and low human well-being are virtually synonymous on Table 13.1. Twelve of the 15 nations listed as having the lowest human well-being also have the lowest GDP/Capita. Extreme poverty places these nations in the lowest level of Maslow's hierarchy of human needs, the physiological needs.[1] When afflicted by this lowly status, Maslow claims all human efforts are directed to survival, and other human needs are postponed. Millennium goals of the United Nations will never be met by the targeted date of 2015 according to this data.

Table 13.1. Comparison of GDP/Capita (PPP) VS 4 Systems Index, 2010

Country	GDP/C	World Rank	Country	4 Systems
Singapore	$62,200	1	Norway	35
Norway	59,100	2	Denmark	40
Kuwait	51,700	3	Australia	45
U.S.A.	47,400	4	Ireland	49
Switzerland	42,900	5	Finland	53
Australia	41,300	6	Spain	63
Netherlands	40,500	7	New Zealand	73
Austria	40,300	8	Netherlands	87
U.A.E.	40,200	9	Austria	91
Canada	39,600	10	France	92
Sweden	39,000	11	Greece	94
Belgium	37,900	12	S. Korea	97
Ireland	37,600	13	Slovakia	99
Denmark	37,000	14	Czech Rep	104
Germany	35,900	15	Sweden	104
Malawi	900	137	Liberia	490
Mozambique	900	138	Myanmar	491
Sierra Leone	900	139	Ethiopia	494
Togo	900	140	Guinea-Bissau	498
Rwanda	900	141	Mozambique	500
Afghanistan	800	142	Rwanda	501
Cent Af Rep	700	143	Cent Af Rep	502
Eritrea	700	144	Burundi	520
Niger	700	145	Niger	524
Guinea-Bissau	600	146	Zimbabwe	525
Somalia	600	147	Eritrea	536
Liberia	500	148	Guinea	542
Burundi	300	149	Somalia	557
Congo Zaire	300	150	Afghanistan	561
Zimbabwe	100	151	Congo Zaire	561

Sources: Tables Ap.3 and Ap.5, Statistical Appendix

Newsweek's conclusions about the world's best countries state:

> …tend to be small, rich, safe, and cold (check out the Nordics in the top 10)…[2]

This article also implies that its "best countries" tend to be the "Happiest Countries." But a look at Table 13.2 is a little unsettling. Suicide is the ultimate "drop out" from society. The list of nations with top suicide rates contain many of the world's richest nations, especially those Nordic countries *Newsweek* and the 4 Systems Index deem to have the highest human well-being. Note that the world mean is 10 suicides per 100,000 population. All the nations listed on Table 13.2 have at least twice the world rate of suicides. Psychologists have suggested that long periods of darkness depress the human psyche and lead to suicide. Another reason for suicide is stressful situations, which seem to abound in highly competitive societies. This discussion is well beyond the scope of this book, but it is mentioned here to convince the reader that human well-being is certainly a complex issue.

As a final thought about the world's human well-being, status and trends of nations, we may take a look at Table 13.3, Net Migration Rates.

> Western nations have many faults, but as I always used to say, there's a simple test of a country: are people trying to get in or out of it? [3]

El Salvador, Lesotho, Saudi Arabia, Trinidad and Tobago, Jamaica, Mali, Sierra Leone, Georgia, Armenia, and Albania lead the world in their citizens seeking havens in other nations of the world. Afghanistan's high net gain in migration is probably due to the closing of refugee camps in Iran and the forced repatriation of about 1 million Afghans into Afghanistan. High gains in immigration can mostly be explained by economic opportunity in the receiving country. Jobs and improvements in economic status are obvious draws for those nations receiving new migrants.

Table 13.2
World Health Organization List of Suicides per 100,000 Population

Rank	Country	Suicides	Rank	Country	Suicides
1	Belarus	74	16	Belgium	37
2	Lithuania	64	17	Croatia	37
3	Russia	63	18	Switzerland	35
4	Sri Lanka	61	19	France	35
5	Kazakhstan	55	20	Uruguay	32
6	Hungary	54	21	Moldova	32
7	Japan	50	22	Poland	31
8	Ukraine	48	23	Austria	31
9	Guyana	45	24	Hong Kong	31
10	S. Korea	44	25	Suriname	29
11	Slovenia	43	26	China	28*
12	Estonia	43	27	Czech Rep	27
13	Latvia	42	28	Sweden	26
14	Serbia	40	29	Bulgaria	26
15	Finland	39	30	Slovakia	26
	World Mean = 10		42	U.S.A.	22

** China is the only nation in which female suicides exceed male suicides*
Source: UNWHO.org

Table 13.3
Net Migration Rates per 100,000 Population

Country	Loss	World Rank	Country	Gain
El Salvador	9.13	1	U.A.E.	21.71
Lesotho	8.68	2	Kuwait	15.65
Saudi Arabia	8.26	3	Australia	6.13
Trinidad & Tob	7.11	4	Canada	5.64
Jamaica	5.52	5	Botswana	4.91
Mali	5.38	6	Singapore	4.79
Sierra Leone	4.66	7	Ireland	4.66
Georgia	4.16	8	U.S.A.	4.25
Armenia	4.16	9	Afghanistan	4.24
Albania	4.15	10	Burundi	4.06
Chad	3.95	11	Portugal	3.06
Morocco	3.88	12	Denmark	2.47
Mexico	3.38	13	Netherlands	2.38
Estonia	3.29	14	Greece	2.33
Kazakhstan	3.28	15	New Zealand	2.30
S. Africa	3.13	16	Israel	2.22
Uzbekistan	2.84	17	Germany	2.19
Jordan	2.81	18	U.K.	2.15
Bulgaria	2.80	19	Italy	2.07
Zambia	2.61	20	Austria	1.83
Krygyzstan	2.58	21	Norway	1.70
Latvia	2.32	22	Sweden	1.65
Gabon	2.24	23	Croatia	1.59
Iran	2.17	24	France	1.47
Guatemala	2.17	25	Pakistan	1.46
Dominican Rep	2.04	25	Switzerland	1.31
Bangladesh	1.97	26	Belgium	1.22
Turkmenistan	1.95	27	Costa Rica	1.11
Haiti	1.95	28	Rwanda	1.11
Cuba	1.56	29	Angola	1.05

Source: CIA World Factbook, 2011.

Table 11.1 shows China's great growth spurt over the past 25 years in Agricultural Value-Added, lowering its Infant Mortality Rate, and raising its GDP/Capita rate. Henry Kissinger has engaged China's top leaders in diplomatic consultations/negotiations for more than 40 years. He describes his contacts from opening U.S.A.—China relations in the 1970s to solidifying cooperative efforts in 2010 to create the conditions for world peace and progress. He believes China's unprecedented growth to be largely the result of Globalization (a concept totally rejected by Mao Zedong in 1970) and the exploitation of China's huge pool of young unskilled labor.

> Propelled by increasing standards of living and longevity combined with the distortion of the one child policy China has one of the world's most rapidly aging populations. The country's working-age population is expected to peak in 2015. From this point on, a shrinking number of Chinese citizens aged fifteen to sixty-four need to support an increasingly large elder population.[4]

As the world's only two economic super-powers of the future, Kissinger projects the concept that China and the U.S.A. are mutually bound by self-interest to work together to promote Human Well-Being throughout the world. A step in this direction might be for them to urge the creation of a "Pacific Community" (WELL NAMED!), similar to the existing "Atlantic Community," whose high levels of Human Well-Being have been well-chronicled in this book.[5]

ENDNOTES

1. See: Maslow, Abraham, *Motivation and Personality*, New York: Harper and Row, 1954.

2. Foroohar, Rana, "The Best Countries in the World," *Newsweek*, August 23 & 30, 2010, p. 32.

3. Blair, Tony, *A Journey: My Political Life*, New York: Alfred A. Knopf, 2010, p. 364.

4. Kissinger, Henry, *On China*, New York: The Penguin Press, 2011, p. 525.

5. Kissinger, Henry, Ibid., p. 528.

Statistical Appendix

Tables

*Table Ap.1 Agriculture Value Added Per Capita, in PPP, 1960-2010**

1960			2010	
Country	VA/C	World Rank	Country	VA/C
U.A.E	$1,257	1	Ireland	$2,110
Japan	945	2	Denmark	1,656
New Zealand	851	3	Malaysia	1,495
Switzerland	828	4	Australia	1,474
Finland	795	5	Romania	1,426
Australia	685	6	Iran	1,406
Gabon	660	7	Serbia	1,321
Canada	655	8	Albania	1,298
Turkey	643	9	Norway	1,250
Norway	593	10	Croatia	1,232
Papua N G	566	11	New Zealand	1,229
Syria	519	12	Uruguay	1,207
Sweden	508	13	Finland	1,204
France	495	14	Spain	1,146
Georgia	478	15	Congo Rep	1,110
Oman	477	16	Armenia	1,097
Croatia	477	17	Greece	1,091
Lebanon	472	18	Belarus	1,079
Turkmenistan	467	19	Macedonia	1,071
Kuwait	448	20	Slovakia	1,060
Greece	432	21	Turkey	1,053
Malaysia	413	22	Thailand	996
Uruguay	407	23	Bulgaria	945
Swaziland	406	24	Chad	915
Uzbekistan	398	25	Paraguay	914
Panama	378	26	Syria	874
Estonia	374	27	Dominican Rep	872
Spain	365	28	Tunisia	872
Slovenia	362	29	Morocco	865
Argentina	359	30	Angola	854
Guatemala	358	31	S. Korea	840
Italy	356	32	Colombia	837
Albania	349	33	Nigeria	794
Mauritius	339	34	El Salvador	788
Moldova	339	35	Egypt	786
Saudi Arabia	334	36	Russia	785
Austria	329	37	Poland	782
Nicaragua	322	38	Papua N G	782
Portugal	317	39	Timor L'Este	773
S. Korea	314	40	Kazakhstan	755
Denmark	312	41	Gabon	751

1960			2010	
Country	VA/C	World Rank	Country	VA/C
Namibia	299	42	Panama	750
Kazakhstan	298	43	Sudan	750
Mexico	291	44	Uzbekistan	750
Colombia	285	45	Netherlands	745
U.S.A.	279	46	Israel	738
Lithuania	278	47	China	719
Tanzania	276	48	Costa Rica	709
El Salvador	273	49	Chile	706
Netherlands	267	50	Peru	705
Belarus	267	51	Czech Rep	703
Mauritania	265	52	Guatemala	702
Azerbaijan	262	53	Argentina	690
Ecuador	259	54	Turkmenistan	690
Poland	254	55	France	689
Tajikistan	248	56	Lithuania	678
Armenia	239	57	Mongolia	678
Macedonia	232	58	Sierra Leone	675
Romania	231	59	Austria	670
Germany	227	60	Lebanon	668
Morocco	224	61	Brazil	663
Costa Rica	220	62	Saudi Arabia	653
Jamaica	220	63	Krygyzstan	645
Egypt	219	64	Bosnia & Herz	643
Hungary	216	65	Ukraine	640
Mongolia	214	66	Libya	638
Bulgaria	210	67	Italy	636
Dominican Rep	209	68	Portugal	632
Serbia	209	69	Hungary	632
Latvia	208	70	Laos	628
Laos	201	71	Canada	614
Cote D'Ivoire	197	72	Azerbaijan	603
Timor L'Este	190	73	Vietnam	600
Cameroon	190	74	Honduras	596
Cambodia	185	75	Algeria	589
Ukraine	185	76	Sweden	589
Russia	176	77	Mauritius	583
Uganda	173	78	Sri Lanka	576
Iraq	172	79	Indonesia	576
Krygyzstan	170	80	Estonia	561
Slovakia	169	81	Ghana	560
Venezuela	167	82	Slovenia	558
Belgium	167	83	U.S.A.	557
Brazil	165	84	Cambodia	551

1960			2010	
Country	VA/C	World Rank	Country	VA/C
Czech Rep	163	85	Namibia	544
Chile	162	86	India	542
Paraguay	161	87	Pakistan	541
U.K.	160	88	Mexico	540
Tunisia	159	89	Mali	540
Cent Af Rep	149	90	Georgia	532
Algeria	148	91	Venezuela	524
Peru	147	92	Japan	522
Nigeria	146	93	Latvia	522
Philippines	145	94	Bolivia	520
Bolivia	143	95	Ecuador	503
Bosnia & Herz	142	96	Oman	502
Gambia	138	97	Swaziland	502
Sudan	137	98	Moldova	501
Zimbabwe	137	99	Switzerland	500
Kenya	136	100	Nicaragua	498
Angola	134	101	Benin	498
Niger	134	102	Philippines	492
Iran	130	103	Taiwan	477
Honduras	128	104	Cote D'Ivoire	476
Vietnam	127	105	Myanmar	472
Guinea-Bissau	127	106	U.A.E.	462
Ghana	126	107	Cameroon	455
Singapore	126	108	N. Korea	443
Senegal	123	109	Togo	427
Madagascar	121	110	U.K	422
Guinea	120	111	Nepal	420
Ethiopia	119	112	Cuba	417
Yemen	115	113	Gambia	409
Benin	113	114	Jamaica	407
Chad	102	115	Ethiopia	394
Sri Lanka	102	116	Somalia	390
Lesotho	101	117	Cent Af Rep	385
S. Africa	100	118	Liberia	385
Congo Zaire	99	119	Rwanda	383
Bangladesh	98	120	Tanzania	372
Thailand	97	121	Guinea-Bissau	372
Zambia	93	122	Haiti	364
Togo	90	123	S. Africa	354
Nepal	90	124	Burkina Faso	353
Mali	89	125	Iraq	346
India	86	126	Kenya	342
Burkina Faso	86	127	Tajikistan	340

1960			2010	
Country	VA/C	World Rank	Country	VA/C
Pakistan	83	128	Malawi	320
Eritrea	83	129	Germany	307
Rwanda	78	130	Bangladesh	299
Indonesia	77	131	Belgium	293
Congo Rep	74	132	Uganda	289
Trinidad & Tob	72	133	Zambia	288
Botswana	70	134	Niger	273
Mozambique	68	135	Lesotho	273
Jordan	53	136	Madagascar	266
Malawi	51	137	Mauritania	263
China	47	138	Afghanistan	248
Burundi	43	139	Yemen	243
		140	Guinea	238
		141	Senegal	221
		142	Mozambique	216
		143	Botswana	210
		144	Jordan	196
		145	Congo Zaire	165
		146	Kuwait	162
		147	Eritrea	121
		148	Trinidad & Tob	116
		149	Burundi	100
		150	Singapore	50
		151	Zimbabwe	19

1960 Mean = $261 2010 Mean = $638

** Sources: 1960:Nationmaster.com; 2010: CIA: 2011*

Table Ap.2. Infant Mortality Rates Per 100,000 Live Births, 1960- 2010

1960			2010	
Country	Rate	World Rank	Country	Rate
Sweden	16	1	Singapore	2
Netherlands	18	2	Sweden	3
Norway	19	3	Japan	3
Australia	20	4	France	3
Czech Rep	22	5	Finland	4
Denmark	22	6	Norway	4
Finland	22	7	Czech Rep	4
New Zealand	22	8	Germany	4
Switzerland	22	9	Switzerland	4
U.K.	23	10	Spain	4
U.S.A.	26	11	Israel	4
Canada	28	12	Slovenia	4
France	29	13	S. Korea	4
Belgium	31	14	Denmark	4
Ireland	31	15	Austria	4
Japan	31	16	Belgium	4
Singapore	31	17	Netherlands	5
Israel	32	18	Australia	5
Slovakia	33	19	Portugal	5
Germany	34	20	U.K.	5
Latvia	35	21	New Zealand	5
Austria	37	22	Canada	5
Belarus	37	23	Ireland	5
Slovenia	37	24	Greece	5
Cuba	39	25	Taiwan	5
Estonia	40	26	Italy	6
Ukraine	41	27	Cuba	6
Italy	44	28	U.S.A.	6
Spain	46	29	Croatia	6
Russia	48	30	Belarus	6
Uruguay	48	31	Lithuania	7
Bulgaria	49	32	Serbia	7
Taiwan	50	33	Poland	7
Hungary	51	34	Slovakia	7
Georgia	52	35	Estonia	7
Lithuania	52	36	Chile	8
Greece	53	37	Hungary	8
Jamaica	56	38	Latvia	9
Venezuela	56	39	Costa Rica	9
Panama	58	40	Kuwait	9
Argentina	60	41	Ukraine	9

1960			2010	
Country	Rate	World Rank	Country	Rate
Trinidad & Tob	61	42	Macedonia	9
Poland	62	43	Bosnia & Herz	9
Moldova	64	44	Russia	11
Lebanon	65	45	Uruguay	11
Paraguay	66	46	Argentina	11
Mauritius	67	47	Saudi Arabia	12
Romania	69	48	Mauritius	12
Croatia	70	49	Botswana	13
Vietnam	70	50	Panama	13
Malaysia	73	51	U.A.E.	13
Armenia	75	52	Moldova	13
Colombia	79	53	Jamaica	15
Philippines	80	54	Malaysia	16
Portugal	81	55	Georgia	16
Sri Lanka	83	56	Syria	17
N. Korea	85	57	Oman	17
Costa Rica	87	58	Colombia	17
Serbia	87	59	Jordan	17
Kuwait	89	60	Thailand	18
S. Korea	90	61	Bulgaria	18
Mexico	94	62	Mexico	18
Tajikistan	95	63	Sri Lanka	19
Jordan	97	64	Albania	19
Zimbabwe	97	65	Armenia	20
Kazakhstan	100	66	China	20
Dominican Rep	102	67	Philippines	21
Thailand	103	68	Ecuador	21
Bosnia & Herz	105	69	El Salvador	22
Ecuador	107	70	Venezuela	22
Albania	112	71	Honduras	22
Madagascar	112	72	Libya	22
Brazil	115	73	Lebanon	22
Iraq	117	74	Vietnam	22
Botswana	118	75	Tunisia	23
Chile	118	76	Brazil	23
Macedonia	120	77	Romania	23
Mongolia	120	78	Uzbekistan	23
Kenya	122	79	Paraguay	25
Rwanda	122	80	Nicaragua	25
Sudan	123	81	Kazakhstan	26
Gabon	125	82	Turkey	26
Zambia	126	83	Dominican Rep	26
Ghana	127	84	Egypt	27

1960			2010	
Country	Rate	World Rank	Country	Rate
Indonesia	128	85	Algeria	28
Namibia	129	86	Guatemala	28
Cambodia	130	87	Peru	29
El Salvador	130	88	Morocco	30
Nicaragua	130	89	Trinidad & Tob	30
S. Africa	130	90	Indonesia	30
Morocco	132	91	Kyrgyzstan	31
Uganda	133	92	Zimbabwe	32
Krygyzstan	135	93	Iran	36
Guatemala	136	94	Mongolia	40
Lesotho	136	95	Timor L'Este	41
Syria	136	96	Tajikistan	41
Honduras	137	97	Eritrea	43
Pakistan	139	98	S. Africa	44
Peru	142	99	Iraq	45
Tanzania	142	100	Bolivia	45
Congo Rep	143	101	Turkmenistan	45
Papua N G	143	102	Namibia	46
U.A.E.	145	103	Papua N G	46
India	146	104	Nepal	48
Burundi	148	105	Myanmar	48
Bangladesh	149	106	India	51
China	150	107	Ghana	51
Swaziland	150	108	N. Korea	51
Uzbekistan	150	109	Gabon	52
Cameroon	151	110	Madagascar	54
Bolivia	152	111	Azerbaijan	55
Laos	155	112	Kenya	55
Togo	158	113	Cambodia	55
Libya	159	114	Togo	57
Myanmar	161	115	Yemen	58
Turkey	163	116	Senegal	59
Algeria	164	117	Bangladesh	59
Iran	164	118	Haiti	60
Oman	164	119	Cameroon	63
Nigeria	165	120	Mauritania	63
Haiti	169	121	Benin	65
Saudi Arabia	170	122	Uganda	65
Tunisia	170	123	Burundi	65
Senegal	173	124	Guinea	65
Congo Zaire	174	125	Rwanda	67
Benin	176	126	Pakistan	67
Ethiopia	180	127	Cote D'Ivoire	68

1960			2010	
Country	Rate	World Rank	Country	Rate
Mauritania	180	128	Gambia	69
Mozambique	180	129	Tanzania	69
Burkina Faso	181	130	Swaziland	70
Egypt	186	131	Lesotho	77
Cent Af Rep	187	132	Laos	78
Liberia	190	133	Congo Rep	80
Eritrea	191	134	Cent Af Rep	81
Cote D'Ivoire	195	135	Ethiopia	81
Azerbaijan	200	136	Congo Zaire	81
Timor L'Este	200	137	Sierra Leone	82
Turkmenistan	200	138	Sudan	82
Malawi	205	139	Burkina Faso	85
Gambia	207	140	Malawi	86
Angola	208	141	Nigeria	94
Guinea-Bissau	211	142	Chad	99
Niger	211	143	Guinea-Bissau	100
Nepal	212	144	Zambia	101
Guinea	215	145	Mozambique	106
Sierra Leone	220	146	Somalia	109
Yemen	225	147	Mali	116
Afghanistan	245	148	Niger	117
Chad	250	149	Liberia	138
Somalia	250	150	Afghanistan	153
Mali	285	151	Angola	180

1960 Mean = 113 2010 Mean = 30

** Sources: 1960: UNICEF.org; 2010: CIA 2011*

*Table Ap.3. GDP/Capita (PPP), 1960- 2010 * ***

1960			2010	
Country	GDP	World Rank	Country	GDP
Kuwait	94,263	1	Singapore	62,200
Switzerland	19,059	2	Norway	59,100
U.S.A.	15,374	3	Kuwait	51,700
Canada	12,701	4	U.S.A.	47,400
Norway	12,509	5	Switzerland	42,900
Denmark	12,280	6	Australia	41,300
Netherlands	12,242	7	Netherlands	40,500
New Zealand	12,186	8	Austria	40,300
U.K.	12,167	9	U.A.E.	40,200
Germany	12,091	10	Canada	39,600
Australia	11,898	11	Sweden	39,000
Sweden	11,183	12	Belgium	37,900
Austria	10,084	13	Ireland	37,600
Belgium	10,077	14	Denmark	37,000
U.A.E.	10,000	15	Germany	35,900
Czech Rep	9,764	16	Finland	35,300
Saudi Arabia	9,727	17	U.K.	35,100
France	9,641	18	Taiwan	35,100
Venezuela	8,714	19	Japan	34,200
Finland	8,563	20	France	33,300
Iraq	7,501	21	Italy	30,700
Italy	7,315	22	Greece	30,200
Slovakia	7,206	23	S. Korea	30,200
Slovenia	7,092	24	Israel	29,500
Argentina	6,985	25	Spain	29,500
Hungary	6,954	26	Slovenia	28,400
Israel	6,291	27	New Zealand	28,000
Ireland	6,125	28	Oman	25,800
Serbia	6,026	29	Czech Rep	25,600
Uruguay	5,721	30	Saudi Arabia	24,200
S. Africa	5,546	31	Portugal	23,000
Japan	5,489	32	Slovakia	22,200
Gabon	5,440	33	Trinidad & Tob	22,100
Lebanon	5,417	34	Estonia	19,000
Greece	5,409	35	Hungary	19,000
Croatia	5,248	36	Poland	18,800
Cuba	5,195	37	Croatia	17,500
Poland	5,138	38	Lithuania	15,900
Jamaica	5,114	39	Russia	15,900
Libya	4,903	40	Chile	15,500
Trinidad & Tob	4,796	41	Argentina	15,000

1960			2010	
Country	GDP	World Rank	Country	GDP
Peru	4,486	42	Malaysia	14,700
Mexico	4,433	43	Gabon	14,600
Romania	4,349	44	Latvia	14,500
Chile	4,322	45	Lebanon	14,200
Spain	4,306	46	Libya	13,800
Portugal	4,196	47	Mexico	13,800
Iran	4,014	48	Uruguay	13,600
Ecuador	4,012	49	Mauritius	13,500
Angola	4,006	50	Belarus	13,400
Armenia	4,000	51	Botswana	13,100
Azerbaijan	4,000	52	Bulgaria	12,800
Belarus	4,000	53	Panama	12,700
Estonia	4,000	54	Venezuela	12,600
Kazakhstan	4,000	55	Kazakhstan	12,500
Latvia	4,000	56	Turkey	12,300
Lithuania	4,000	57	Romania	11,500
Moldova	4,000	58	Costa Rica	11,400
Russia	4,000	59	Iran	11,200
Turkmenistan	4,000	60	Azerbaijan	11,000
Ukraine	4,000	61	Serbia	11,000
Uzbekistan	4,000	62	Brazil	10,900
Bulgaria	3,759	63	S. Africa	10,700
Algeria	3,717	64	Cuba	9,900
El Salvador	3,469	65	Colombia	9,800
Singapore	3,426	66	Tunisia	9,500
Costa Rica	3,375	67	Macedonia	9,400
Nicaragua	3,248	68	Peru	9,200
Macedonia	3,207	69	Angola	8,700
Panama	3,120	70	Thailand	8,700
Brazil	3,044	71	Dominican Rep	8,600
Krygyzstan	3,000	72	Jamaica	8,400
Tajikistan	3,000	73	Albania	8,000
Timor L'Este	3,000	74	Ecuador	7,800
Namibia	2,893	75	Algeria	7,400
Georgia	2,720	76	China	7,400
Guatemala	2,697	77	Turkmenistan	7,400
Oman	2,523	78	El Salvador	7,300
Congo Rep	2,417	79	Namibia	6,900
Colombia	2,399	80	Ukraine	6,700
Turkey	2,273	81	Bosnia & Herz	6,600
Honduras	2,262	82	Egypt	6,200
Albania	2,220	83	Armenia	5,800
Mauritius	2,161	84	Jordan	5,300

1960			2010	
Country	GDP	World Rank	Country	GDP
Bolivia	2,118	85	Guatemala	5,200
Jordan	2,088	86	Morocco	4,900
Paraguay	2,016	87	Sri Lanka	4,900
Sudan	1,936	88	Paraguay	4,900
Malaysia	1,904	89	Bolivia	4,800
Haiti	1,781	90	Syria	4,800
Syria	1,754	91	Georgia	4,800
Taiwan	1,680	92	Swaziland	4,500
Bosnia & Herz	1,638	93	Indonesia	4,300
Madagascar	1,638	94	Congo Rep	4,200
Cote D'Ivoire	1,623	95	Honduras	4,200
Tunisia	1,616	96	Iraq	3,600
Senegal	1,608	97	Philippines	3,500
N. Korea	1,597	98	India	3.400
Philippines	1,585	99	Mongolia	3,300
Egypt	1,563	100	Uzbekistan	3,100
Dominican Rep	1,553	101	Vietnam	3,100
Zambia	1,541	102	Nicaragua	2,900
Morocco	1,537	103	Pakistan	2,600
S. Korea	1,513	104	Yemen	2,500
Swaziland	1,429	105	Papua N G	2,400
Cameroon	1,386	106	Nigeria	2,400
Chad	1,349	107	Timor L'Este	2,400
Somalia	1,304	108	Cameroon	2,300
Cent Af Rep	1,225	109	Sudan	2,300
Ghana	1,159	110	Moldova	2,300
Papua N G	1,120	111	Kyrgyzstan	2,100
Nigeria	1,105	112	Laos	2,100
Sierra Leone	1,081	113	Mauritania	2,100
Sri Lanka	1,072	114	N. Korea	1,900
Togo	1,011	115	Cambodia	1,900
Benin	997	116	Tajikistan	1,800
Mongolia	997	117	Lesotho	1,700
Botswana	953	118	Cote D'Ivoire	1,700
Mauritania	946	119	Chad	1,600
Thailand	940	120	Bangladesh	1,600
Kenya	928	121	Kenya	1,600
Niger	903	122	Senegal	1,600
Congo Zaire	874	123	Benin	1,500
Afghanistan	869	124	Ghana	1,500
Laos	857	125	Zambia	1,500
Indonesia	835	126	Gambia	1,400
Yemen	816	127	Tanzania	1,400

1960			2010	
Country	GDP	World Rank	Country	GDP
Uganda	789	128	Haiti	1,300
Pakistan	744	129	Uganda	1,300
Tanzania	709	130	Mali	1,200
Vietnam	697	131	Burkina Faso	1,200
Bangladesh	679	132	Nepal	1,200
Burkina Faso	662	133	Myanmar	1,100
India	654	134	Madagascar	1,000
Liberia	645	135	Guinea	900
Nepal	641	136	Ethiopia	900
Guinea	621	137	Malawi	900
China	592	138	Mozambique	900
Rwanda	564	139	Sierra Leone	900
Gambia	554	140	Togo	900
Mozambique	528	141	Rwanda	900
Zimbabwe	527	142	Afghanistan	800
Mali	511	143	Cent Af Rep	700
Cambodia	490	144	Eritrea	700
Guinea-Bissau	465	145	Niger	700
Malawi	429	146	Guinea-Bissau	600
Ethiopia	399	147	Somalia	600
Burundi	397	148	Liberia	500
Myanmar	371	149	Burundi	300
Lesotho	364	150	Congo Zaire	300
Eritrea	363	151	Zimbabwe	100

1960 Mean = 4,384 2010 Mean = 12,575

** In 1960, all Soviet Republics were assigned a GNP of $4,000*

*** Sources: 1960 Gapminder.com; 2010 CIA Estimates*

*Table Ap.4. Civil and Political Liberties, 2 is Best, 14 is Worst, 1972- 2010 **

1972			2010	
Country	Liberties	World Rank	Country	Liberties
Australia	2	1	Australia	2
Austria	2	2	Austria	2
Belgium	2	3	Belgium	2
Canada	2	4	Canada	2
Costa Rica	2	5	Chile	2
Denmark	2	6	Costa Rica	2
Germany	2	7	Czech Rep	2
Japan	2	8	Denmark	2
Netherlands	2	9	Estonia	2
New Zealand	2	10	Finland	2
Norway	2	11	France	2
Sweden	2	12	Germany	2
Switzerland	2	13	Hungary	2
U.K.	2	14	Ireland	2
U.S.A.	2	15	Lithuania	2
France	3	16	Netherlands	2
Ireland	3	17	New Zealand	2
Italy	3	18	Norway	2
Jamaica	3	19	Poland	2
Argentina	4	20	Portugal	2
Colombia	4	21	Slovakia	2
Finland	4	22	Slovenia	2
Gambia	4	23	Spain	2
Guatemala	4	24	Sweden	2
Lebanon	4	25	Switzerland	2
S. Korea	4	26	U.K	2
Trinidad & Tob	4	27	U.S.A.	2
Venezuela	4	28	Uruguay	2
Botswana	5	29	Croatia	3
Dominican Rep	5	30	Ghana	3
El Salvador	5	31	Greece	3
India	5	32	Israel	3
Israel	5	33	Italy	3
Malaysia	5	34	Japan	3
Mauritius	5	35	Mauritius	3
Sri Lanka	5	36	Panama	3
Turkey	6	37	S. Korea	3
Burkina Faso	7	38	Taiwan	3
Kuwait	7	39	Argentina	4
Mexico	7	40	Benin	4
Bangladesh	8	41	Brazil	4

1972			2010	
Country	Liberties	World Rank	Country	Liberties
Lesotho	8	42	Bulgaria	4
Pakistan	8	43	Dominican Rep	4
Bolivia	9	44	Latvia	4
Honduras	9	45	Mongolia	4
Kenya	9	46	Namibia	4
Madagascar	9	47	Romania	4
Nicaragua	9	48	Serbia	4
Thailand	9	49	S. Africa	4
S. Africa	9	50	Trinidad & Tob	4
Brazil	10	51	Botswana	5
Cameroon	10	52	El Salvador	5
Indonesia	10	53	India	5
Laos	10	54	Indonesia	5
Morocco	10	55	Jamaica	5
Nigeria	10	56	Mali	5
Paraguay	10	57	Peru	5
Philippines	10	58	Albania	5
Singapore	10	59	Bolivia	5
Swaziland	10	60	Ecuador	6
Uruguay	10	61	Lesotho	6
Zambia	10	62	Macedonia	6
Cambodia	11	64	Mexico	6
Congo Rep	11	65	Moldova	6
Ecuador	11	66	Paraguay	6
Ethiopia	11	67	Philippines	6
Iran	11	68	Senegal	6
Liberia	11	69	Sierra Leone	7
Namibia	11	70	Tanzania	7
Nepal	11	71	Turkey	7
Portugal	11	72	Ukraine	7
Sierra Leone	11	73	Bangladesh	7
Spain	11	74	Bosnia & Herz	7
Taiwan	11	75	Colombia	7
Tunisia	11	76	Georgia	7
U.A.E.	11	77	Kenya	7
Zimbabwe	11	78	Liberia	7
Algeria	12	79	Malawi	7
Benin	12	80	Mozambique	7
Chile	12	81	Papua N G	7
Cote D'Ivoire	12	82	Timor L'Este	7
Egypt	12	83	Zambia	7
Gabon	12	84	Burkina Faso	8
Greece	12	85	Guatemala	8

1972			2010	
Country	Liberties	World Rank	Country	Liberties
Haiti	12	86	Guinea-Bissau	8
Hungary	12	87	Honduras	8
Jordan	12	88	Lebanon	8
Mauritania	12	89	Malaysia	8
Niger	12	90	Nepal	8
Poland	12	91	Nigeria	8
Saudi Arabia	12	92	Haiti	9
Senegal	12	93	Kuwait	9
Sudan	12	94	Morocco	9
Tanzania	12	95	Niger	9
Togo	12	96	Pakistan	9
Afghanistan	13	97	Singapore	9
Chad	13	98	Sri Lanka	9
Congo Zaire	13	99	Thailand	9
Ghana	13	100	Togo	9
Malawi	13	101	Uganda	9
Mali	13	102	Armenia	10
Oman	13	103	Burundi	10
Panama	13	104	Cent Af Rep	10
Romania	13	105	Gambia	10
Rwanda	13	106	Guinea	10
Somalia	13	107	Kyrgyzstan	10
Albania	14	108	Madagascar	10
Angola	14	109	Venezuela	10
Armenia	14	110	Algeria	11
Azerbaijan	14	111	Angola	11
Belarus	14	112	Azerbaijan	11
Bosnia & Herz	14	113	Cambodia	11
Bulgaria	14	114	Congo Rep	11
Burundi	14	115	Egypt	11
Cent Af Rep	14	116	Gabon	11
China	14	117	Iraq	11
Croatia	14	118	Jordan	11
Cuba	14	119	Kazakhstan	11
Czech Rep	14	120	Mauritania	11
Eritrea	14	121	Oman	11
Estonia	14	122	Russia	11
Georgia	14	123	Rwanda	11
Guinea-Bissau	14	124	Tajikistan	11
Guinea	14	125	U.A.E.	11
Iraq	14	126	Yemen	11
Kazakhstan	14	127	Afghanistan	12
Krygyzstan	14	128	Cameroon	12

1972			2010	
Country	Liberties	World Rank	Country	Liberties
Latvia	14	129	CongoZaire	12
Lithuania	14	130	Iran	12
Libya	14	131	Ethiopia	12
Macedonia	14	132	Swaziland	12
Moldova	14	133	Tunisia	12
Mongolia	14	134	Vietnam	12
Mozambique	14	135	Zimbabwe	12
Myanmar	14	136	Belarus	13
N. Korea	14	137	Chad	13
Papua N G	14	138	China	13
Russia	14	139	Cote D'Ivoire	13
Serbia	14	140	Cuba	13
Slovakia	14	141	Laos	13
Slovenia	14	142	Saudi Arabia	13
Syria	14	143	Syria	14
Tajikistan	14	144	Eritrea	14
Timor L'Este	14	145	Libya	14
Turkmenistan	14	146	Myanmar	14
Uganda	14	147	N. Korea	14
Ukraine	14	148	Somalia	14
Uzbekistan	14	149	Sudan	14
Vietnam	14	150	Turkmenistan	14
Yemen	14	151	Uzbekistan	14

1972 Mean = 10 2010 Mean = 7

* *Source: Freedomhouse.org*

Table Ap.5. Four Systems Cumulative World Rankings, 1960-2010

2010		World	1960	
Country	Total Ranks	Rank	Country	Total Ranks
Norway	35	1	Switzerland	21
Denmark #	40	2	New Zealand	26
Australia	45	3	Norway	26
Ireland #	49	4	Australia	29
Finland #	53	5	Canada	32
Spain #	63	6	Sweden	34
New Zealand	73	7	Finland	56
Netherlands #	87	8	Japan	58
Austria #	91	9	Denmark	62
France #	92	10	France #	62
Greece #	94	11	Netherlands #	67
S. Korea	97	12	U.S.A.	68
Slovakia #	99	13	Austria	81
Czech Rep #	104	14	Germany #	98
Sweden #	104	15	Italy #	99
Croatia	109	16	U.K.	115
Israel	114	17	Argentina	120
Canada	116	18	Kuwait	120
Uruguay	119	19	Belgium #	121
Poland #	120	20	Lebanon	121
Switzerland	128	21	Ireland	140
U.S.A.	129	22	Uruguay	141
Slovenia #	132	23	Israel	150
Portugal #	134	24	Jamaica	157
Chile	140	25	Venezuela	164
Lithuania #	142	26	Spain	174
Serbia	146	27	Greece	181
Italy #	149	28	Mexico	188
Hungary #	155	29	U.A.E.	190
Japan	159	30	Malaysia	195
Costa Rica	161	31	Costa Rica	196
Estonia #	162	32	Mauritius	198
U.K. #	165	33	Colombia	202
Belgium #	167	34	Slovenia	205
Germany #	168	35	Gabon	210
Argentina	174	36	Portugal	212
Taiwan	175	37	Hungary	213
Panama	179	38	Poland	224
Bulgaria #	181	39	Guatemala	226
Romania #	184	40	S. Korea	229
Malaysia	187	41	Croatia	232

2010		World	1960	
Country	Total Ranks	Rank	Country	Total Ranks
Macedonia	191	42	El Salvador	235
Mauritius	207	43	Estonia	236
Albania	209	44	Czech Rep	237
Latvia #	211	45	Panama	238
Turkey	223	46	Trinidad & Tob	240
Dominican Rep	225	47	Nicaragua	243
Colombia	230	48	Turkey	243
Belarus	237	49	Ecuador	244
Russia	238	50	Singapore	247
El Salvador	239	51	Slovakia	252
Ukraine	241	52	Romania	253
Brazil	245	53	Georgia	256
Singapore	250	54	Belarus	260
Mexico	251	55	Cuba	263
Thailand	251	56	Moldova	265
Paraguay	256	57	Taiwan	268
Peru	260	58	Dominican Rep	269
Bosnia & Herz	261	59	Lithuania	269
Lebanon	264	60	Namibia	274
Armenia	271	61	Latvia	277
Kuwait	277	62	Paraguay	277
Saudi Arabia	280	63	Brazil	285
U.A.E	286	64	Serbia	286
Jamaica	287	65	S. Africa	286
Iran	289	66	Armenia	289
Kazakhstan	295	67	Ukraine	289
Mongolia	295	68	Bulgaria	294
Botswana	300	69	Russia	294
Oman	300	70	Swaziland	294
Ecuador	301	71	Chile	295
Tunisia	302	72	Kazakhstan	295
Morocco	303	73	Saudi Arabia	300
Guatemala	310	74	Iraq	303
Gabon	311	75	Philippines	304
Namibia	312	76	Morocco	312
Syria	314	77	Oman	314
Trinidad & Tob	315	78	Albania	316
Venezuela	315	79	Sri Lanka	319
Indonesia	316	80	Uzbekistan	319
Sri Lanka	316	81	Tajikistan	321
Timor L'Este	316	82	Peru	322
Egypt	319	83	Madagascar	323
Georgia	322	84	Syria	327

2010		World	1960	
Country	Total Ranks	Rank	Country	Total Ranks
Papua N G	322	85	Honduras	330
Honduras	328	86	Macedonia	334
China	329	87	Bolivia	338
S. Africa	329	88	Iran	340
Libya	333	89	Turkmenistan	342
Moldova	333	90	Cameroon	347
Philippines	342	91	Kenya	347
Ghana	345	92	Papua N G	353
Cuba	346	93	Libya	355
India	346	94	Sudan	355
Bolivia	348	95	N. Korea	356
Algeria	355	96	Thailand	356
Congo Rep	361	97	Algeria	360
Azerbaijan	363	98	Botswana	361
Nicaragua	369	99	Zambia	364
Uzbekistan	370	100	Laos	365
Vietnam	377	101	Tanzania	366
Nigeria	378	102	Azerbaijan	371
Turkmenistan	378	103	Haiti	371
Angola	382	104	Jordan	375
Krygyzstan	384	105	Krygyzstan	375
Benin	392	106	Cambodia	377
Sierra Leone	398	107	Zimbabwe	377
Jordan	404	108	Tunisia	379
Pakistan	414	109	Nigeria	382
Mali	422	110	Egypt	383
Chad	427	111	Congo Rep	384
Cambodia	429	112	Mauritania	387
Nepal	436	113	Bosnia & Herz	388
Sudan	438	114	Cote D'Ivoire	390
Iraq	439	115	Mongolia	390
Bangladesh	443	116	India	397
Senegal	443	117	Pakistan	397
Kenya	446	118	Indonesia	399
Lesotho	448	119	Bangladesh	400
Swaziland	450	120	Gambia	401
Tanzania	451	121	Sierra Leone	402
Laos	454	122	Ghana	403
Tajikistan	457	123	Lesotho	404
Togo	461	124	Liberia	411
Cote D'Ivoire	467	125	Timor L'Este	412
Haiti	467	126	Vietnam	415
Gambia	468	127	Senegal	418

2010		World	1960	
Country	Total Ranks	Rank	Country	Total Ranks
Cameroon	469	128	Angola	421
Yemen	476	129	Niger	424
Zambia	476	130	Uganda	427
N. Korea	480	131	Burkina Faso	429
Burkina Faso	481	132	Somalia	432
Malawi	481	133	Togo	439
Uganda	482	134	Benin	445
Madagascar	486	135	Afghanistan	446
Mauritania	487	136	Rwanda	451
Liberia	490	137	Ethiopia	457
Myanmar	491	138	Cent Af Rep	460
Ethiopia	494	139	Congo Zaire	469
Guinea-Bissau	498	140	Chad	473
Mozambique	500	141	Nepal	475
Rwanda	501	142	Myanmar	478
Cent Af Rep	502	143	China	512
Burundi	520	144	Yemen	516
Niger	524	145	Burundi	521
Zimbabwe	525	146	Mali	521
Eritrea	536	147	Guinea	522
Guinea	542	148	Guinea-Bissau	522
Somalia	557	149	Malawi	524
Afghanistan	561	150	Mozambique	534
Congo Zaire	561	151	Eritrea	543

Sources: Tables Ap.1,Ap.2,Ap.3,Ap.4
 # = Members of European Union

*Table Ap.6. United Nations Human Development Index (HDI), 1975-2010**

Rank	Country	2010 Index	1975 Index	Difference
1	Norway	938	870	+68
2	Australia	937	851	+86
3	New Zealand	907	854	+53
4	U.S.A.	902	870	+32
5	Ireland	895	823	+72
6	Netherlands	890	873	+17
7	Canada	888	873	+15
8	Sweden	885	872	+13
9	Germany	885	863	+22
10	Japan	884	861	+23
11	S. Korea	877	713	+164
12	Switzerland	874	883	-9
13	France	872	856	+16
14	Israel	872	805	+67
15	Finland	871	846	+25
16	Belgium	867	852	+15
17	Denmark	866	875	-9
18	Spain	863	846	+17
19	Greece	855	841	+14
20	Italy	854	845	+9
21	Austria	851	848	+3
22	U.K.	849	853	-4
23	Singapore	846	819 (E)	+27
24	Slovenia	828	819 (E)	+9
25	Taiwan	819 (E)	629 (E)	+190
26	Slovakia	818	819 (E)	-1
27	Cuba	817	819 (E)	-2
28	U.A.E.	815	734	+81
29	Estonia	812	811	+1
30	Hungary	805	786	+19
31	Portugal	795	793	+2
32	Poland	795	768 (E)	+27
33	Lithuania	783	768 (E)	+15
34	Chile	783	708	+75
35	Oman	781	768 (E)	+13
36	Argentina	775	790	-5
37	Kuwait	771	771	0
38	Latvia	769	797	-28
39	Romania	767	786	-19
40	Croatia	767	768	-1
41	Uruguay	765	762	+3
42	Lebanon	759	768 (E)	-9

Rank	Country	2010 Index	1975 Index	Difference
43	Libya	755	768 (E)	-13
44	Panama	755	718	+37
45	Saudi Arabia	752	611	+141
46	Mexico	750	694	+56
47	Malaysia	744	619	+133
48	Bulgaria	743	771	-28
49	Trinidad & Tob	736	756	-20
50	Serbia	735	629 (E)	+160
51	Belarus	732	629 (E)	+103
52	Costa Rica	725	746	-21
53	Peru	723	647	+76
54	Albania	719	675	+44
55	Russia	719	815	-96
56	Kazakhstan	714	629 (E)	+85
57	Azerbaijan	713	629 (E)	+84
58	Bosnia & Herz	710	629 (E)	+81
59	Ukraine	710	629 (E)	+81
60	Iran	702	571	+131
61	Macedonia	701	629 (E)	+72
62	Mauritius	701	662	+19
63	Brazil	699	649	+50
64	Georgia	698	629 (E)	+59
65	Venezuela	696	723	-27
66	Armenia	695	629 (E)	+74
67	Ecuador	695	636	+59
68	Colombia	689	663	+26
69	Jamaica	688	686	+2
70	Tunisia	683	519	+164
71	Jordan	681	647	+34
72	Turkey	679	594	+85
73	Algeria	677	511	+166
74	Turkmenistan	669	629 (E)	+40
75	Dominican Rep	663	628	+35
76	China	663	530	+133
77	El Salvador	659	595	+64
78	Sri Lanka	659	619	+39
79	Thailand	654	615	+39
80	Gabon	648	629 (E)	+19
81	Bolivia	643	519	+124
82	Paraguay	640	667	-27
83	Philippines	638	655	-17
84	Botswana	633	509	+124
85	Moldova	623	629 (E)	-6
86	Mongolia	622	629 (E)	-7

Rank	Country	2010 Index	1975 Index	Difference
87	Egypt	620	434	+186
88	Uzbekistan	617	629 (E)	-12
89	Namibia	606	503 (E)	+103
90	Honduras	604	528	+76
91	Congo Rep	601	503 (E)	+98
92	Indonesia	600	471	+129
93	Krygyzstan	598	503 (E)	+95
94	S. Africa	597	650	-53
95	Syria	589	547	+42
96	Tajikistan	580	503 (E)	+77
97	Vietnam	572	503 (E)	+69
98	Morocco	567	435	+132
99	Nicaragua	565	583	-18
100	Guatemala	560	514	+46
101	Pakistan	527	503 (E)	+24
102	India	519	419	+100
103	Congo Rep	512	503 (E)	+9
104	Iraq	503 (E)	629 (E)	-126
105	Timor L'Este	502	503 (E)	-1
106	Swaziland	498	527	-25
107	Laos	497	503 (E)	-6
108	Cambodia	494	503 (E)	-9
109	Eritrea	472	503 (E)	-31
110	Kenya	470	466	+4
111	Bangladesh	469	347	+122
112	Ghana	467	442	+25
113	Cameroon	460	422	+38
114	Myanmar	451	406 (E)	+45
115	Eritrea	444	406 (E)	+38
116	Yemen	439	406 (E)	+33
117	Benin	435	406 (E)	+29
118	Madagascar	435	407	+28
119	Mauritania	433	383	+50
120	Papua N G	431	431	0
121	Nepal	428	301	+127
122	Togo	428	423	+5
123	Lesotho	427	499	-72
124	Nigeria	423	321	+102
125	Uganda	422	406 (E)	+16
126	Senegal	411	342	+69
127	Somalia	406 (E)	406 (E)	0
128	Haiti	404	442	-38
129	Angola	403	406 (E)	-3
130	Tanzania	398	406 (E)	-8

Rank	Country	2010 Index	1975 Index	Difference
131	Cote D'Ivoire	397	369	+28
132	Zambia	395	449	-54
133	Gambia	390	290	+100
134	Rwanda	385	336	+49
135	Malawi	385	316	+69
136	Sudan	379	354	+25
137	Afghanistan	349	406 (E)	-57
138	Guinea	340	406 (E)	-66
139	Ethiopia	328	406 (E)	-78
140	Sierra Leone	317	406 (E)	-89
141	Cent Af Rep	315	333	-18
142	Mali	309	252	+57
143	Burkina Faso	305	232	+73
144	Liberia	300	406 (E)	-106
145	Chad	295	256	+39
146	Guinea-Bissau	289	248	+41
147	Mozambique	284	406 (E)	-122
148	Burundi	282	280	+2
149	Niger	261	234	+27
150	Congo Zaire	239	406 (E)	-176
151	Zimbabwe	140	550	-410

SOURCE: www.undp.org
(E) = Estimates based on development category of nation; estimates made for missing data.

Table Ap.7. Newsweek*'s "Best Countries"; Veenhoven's Happiest Countries**

Latest Data

Country	Rating	World Rank	Country	Rating
Finland	89	1	Costa Rica	8.5
Switzerland	89	2	Denmark	8.3
Sweden	89	3	Switzerland	8.0
Australia	87	4	Finland	7.9
Luxembourg	87	5	Mexico	7.9
Norway	87	6	Norway	7.9
Canada	87	7	Canada	7.8
Netherlands	86	8	Panama	7.8
Japan	85	9	Sweden	7.8
Denmark	85	10	Australia	7.7
U.S.A.	85	11	Austria	7.7
Germany	84	12	Colombia	7.7
New Zealand	84	13	Dominican Rep	7.6
U.K.	83	14	Ireland	7.6
S. Korea	83	15	Netherlands	7.6
France	83	16	Brazil	7.5
Ireland	83	17	New Zealand	7.4
Austria	82	18	U.S.A.	7.4
Belgium	82	19	Argentina	7.3
Singapore	80	20	Belgium	7.3
Spain	80	21	U.A.E.	7.3
Israel	79	22	Guatemala	7.2
Italy	78	23	Spain	7.2
Slovenia	78	24	Venezuela	7.2
Czech Rep	77	25	Germany	7.1
Greece	76	26	Nicaragua	7.1
Portugal	76	27	U.K.	7.1
Croatia	74	28	Honduras	7.0
Poland	74	29	Israel	7.0
Chile	74	30	Trinidad & Tob	7.0
Slovakia	73	31	Paraguay	6.9
Estonia	73	32	Singapore	6.9
Hungary	72	33	Slovenia	6.9
Lithuania	71	34	Kuwait	6.8
Costa Rica	69	35	Uruguay	6.8
Latvia	69	36	El Salvador	6.7
Malaysia	69	37	Italy	6.7
Bulgaria	69	38	Jamaica	6.7
Romania	68	39	Chile	6.6
Kuwait	68	40	France	6.6
Panama	68	41	Thailand	6.6
Peru	67	42	Bolivia	6.5

Country	Rating	World Rank	Country	Rating
U.A.E.	66	43	Czech Rep	6.5
Uruguay	66	44	Japan	6.5
Mexico	65	45	Malaysia	6.5
Argentina	64	46	Saudi Arabia	6.4
Jamaica	64	47	Ecuador	6.4
Brazil	64	48	Greece	6.4
Ukraine	64	49	Poland	6.3
Cuba	63	50	China	6.3
Russia	63	51	Indonesia	6.3
Turkey	63	52	Laos	6.2
Jordan	62	53	Peru	6.2
Qatar	62	54	Taiwan	6.2
Dominican Rep	62	55	Kazakhstan	6.1
Belarus	62	56	Vietnam	6.1
Albania	62	57	Croatia	6.0
Thailand	62	58	Estonia	6.0
China	62	59	S. Korea	6.0
Oman	61	60	Uzbekistan	6.0
Kazakhstan	61	61	Iran	5.9
Colombia	60	62	Jordan	5.9
Philippines	60	63	Philippines	5.9
Saudi Arabia	59	64	Slovakia	5.9
Tunisia	58	65	Syria	5.9
Sri Lanka	58	66	Tunisia	5.9
Morocco	58	67	S. Africa	5.8
Paraguay	58	68	Nigeria	5.7
Azerbaijan	58	69	Egypt	5.7
Ecuador	58	70	Mongolia	5.7
Venezuela	57	71	Portugal	5.7
El Salvador	57	72	Romania	5.7
Indonesia	57	73	Turkey	5.6
Egypt	57	74	Hungary	5.5
Nicaragua	57	75	India	5.5
Honduras	56	76	Kyrgyzstan	5.5
Bolivia	55	77	Lithuania	5.5
India	55	78	Russia	5.5
Iran	55	79	Algeria	5.4
Botswana	55	80	Chad	5.4
Vietnam	54	81	Latvia	5.4
S. Africa	54	82	Morocco	5.4
Syria	54	83	Azerbaijan	5.3
Guatemala	54	84	Bangladesh	5.3
Algeria	52	85	Bosnia & Herz	5.3
Ghana	49	86	Nepal	5.3

Country	Rating	World Rank	Country	Rating
Kenya	49	87	Belarus	5.2
Bangladesh	47	88	Ghana	5.2
Pakistan	47	89	Namibia	5.2
Madagascar	46	90	Sri Lanka	5.1
Senegal	46	91	Tajikistan	5.1
Yemen	44	92	Armenia	5.0
Tanzania	43	93	Pakistan	5.0
Ethiopia	41	94	Sudan	5.0
Mozambique	41	95	Ukraine	5.0
Uganda	40	96	Zambia	5.0
Zambia	40	97	Cambodia	4.9
Cameroon	38	98	Mauritania	4.9
Nigeria	38	99	Moldova	4.9
Burkina Faso	33	100	Malawi	4.8

* Newsweek *evaluated only 100 countries*
Sources: Foroohar, 2010; worlddatabaseofhappiness.eur.nl

ENDNOTES

1. See: Maslow, Abraham, *Motivation And Personality*, New York: Harper and Row, 1954.

2. Foroohar, Rana, "The Best Countries in the World," *Newsweek*, August 23 & 30, 2010, p. 32.

3. Blair, Tony, A *Journey: My Political Life*, New York: Alfred A. Knopf, 2010, p. 364.

4. Kissinger, Henry, *On China*, New York: The Penguin Press, 2011, p. 525.

5. Kissinger, Henry, Ibid., p. 528.

Bibliography

Aston, Adam, "Can China Clean Up Its Act?" *Businessweek*, May 25, 2009, pp. 41-44.

Ayittey, George, *Africa Unchained. The Blueprint For Development*, New York: Palmgrave/MacMillan, 2005.

Belt, Don, "Shadowland: Poised to Play a Pivotal New Role in the Middle East, Syria Struggles to Escape its Dark Past," *National Geographic*, Vol 216, no. 5, November 2009, pp. 52-75.

Blair, Tony, *A Journey: My Political Life*, New York: Alfred A. Knopf, 2010.

Bok, Derek, *The Politics Of Happiness: What Government Can Learn From The New Research On Well-Being*, Princeton, NJ: Princeton University Press, 2010.

Bourne, Joel K. Jr., "The End of Plenty, Special Report: The Global Food Crisis," *National Geographic*, Vol 215, no. 6, June 2009, pp. 26-59.

Bush, Jason, "Russia: Its Scarier Than You Think," *Businessweek*, October 20, 2008, pp. 44-52.

Carroll, Chris, "Serbs Face the Future," *National Geographic*, Vol 216, no. 1, July 2009, pp. 96-119.

Cascio, Jamais, "Get Smart." *The Atlantic*, Vol 304, no.1, July-August 2009, pp. 94-100.

CIA, *World Factbook 2011*, New York: Skyhorse Publishing, 2010.

CIA, World Factbook: ciaworldfactbook.us

Draper, Robert, "Opium Wars," *National Geographic*, Vol 219 no. 2, Feb 2011, pp. 58-83.

Easterly, William, *The White Man's Burden: Why The West's Efforts To Aid The Rest Have Done So Much Ill And So Little Good*, New York: The Penguin Press, 2006.

Engardio, Pete and Geri Smith, "Business is Standing Its Ground," *Businessweek*, April 20, 2009, pp. 34-39.

Environmental Performance Index: epi.yale.edu

Failed States Index: fundforpeace.org/web/index.php

Fallows, James, "How America Can Rise Again," *The Atlantic*, January/February 2010, pp. 54-61.

Family Information: unicef.org

Finkel, Michael, "Facing Down Fanatics," *National Geographic*, Vol 216, no. 4, October 2009, pp. 76-99.

Foroohar, Rana, "The Best Countries in the World," *Newsweek*, August 23 & 30, 2010, pp. 30-42.

Freedom Information: freedom house.org/research/survey2005

Friedman, Thomas L., *The World Is Flat: A Brief History Of The Twenty-First Century*, New York: Farrar, Straus, and Giroux, 2006.

———, *Hot, Flat, And Crowded: Why We Need A Green Revolution—And How It Can Renew America*, New York: Farrar, Straus, and Giroux, 2008.

Friedman, Thomas L., "Why Americans are No. 11," *The New York Times*, Tuesday, September 14, 2010.

Galbraith, John Kenneth, *The Affluent Society*, Boston: Houghton Mifflin, 1958.

Galbraith, John Kenneth, *A Journey Through Economic Time: A First Hand View*, Boston: Houghton Mifflin, 1994.

General Information: neweconomics.org

Gladwell, Malcom, *Blink: The Power Of Thinking Without Thinking*, New York: Little, Brown and Company 2004.

———, *Outliers: The Story Of Success*, New York: Little, Brown and Company, 2008.

Greenspan, Alan, *The Age Of Turbulence: An Adventure In A New World*, New York: The Penguin Press, 2007.

Halperin, David, *The Hidden Wealth Of Nations*, Cambridge, UK and Malden, MA: Polity Press, 2010.

Hamid, Tawfik, "The Trouble With Islam," *The Wall Street Journal*, Tuesday, April 3, 2007, p. A15.

Hamm, Steve, "The Trouble With India," *Businessweek*, March 19, 2007, pp. 49-58.

Hardin, Garrett, "The Tragedy of the Commons," *Science*, Vol 162 (1968), pp 1243-1248.

Health Expenditures: info please.com/ipa

Held, David, Anthony McGrew, David Goldblatt, and Johnathan Perraton, *Global Transformations: Politics, Economics, And Culture*, Palo Alto: Stanford University Press, 1999.

Hubbard, Glen and William Duggan, *The Aid Trap*, New York: Columbia University Press, 2009.

Human Development: undp.org

Huxley, Aldous, *Brave New World*, New York: The Modern Library, 1932, 1946.

Kagan, Robert, *Of Paradise And Power: America And Europe In The New World Order*. New York: Alfred Knopf, 2003.

Kaplan, Robert D. "Looking the World in the Eye," *The Atlantic*, Vol 288, no.5, December 2001, pp. 68-82.

Kennedy, David M., "What Would Wilson Do?," *The Atlantic*, January/February, 2010, pp. 90-94.

Kissinger, Henry, *Diplomacy*, New York: Simon and Schuster, 1994.

———, *On China*, New York: The Penguin Press, 2011.

Lamb, David, *The Africans*, New York: Random House, 1982.

Lancaster, John, "Pakistan's Heartland Under Threat," *National Geographic*, Vol 218, no. 1, July 2010, pp. 82-107.

Levitt, Steven D and Stephen J. Dubner, *Freakonomics: A Rogue Economist Explores The Hidden Side Of Everything*, New York: Harper Collins, 2005.

Maslow, Abraham, *Motivation And Personality*, New York: Harper and Row, 1954.

McArdle, Megan, "Misleading Indicator: Will The Great Recession Finally End Our Misguided Obsession With Gross Domestic Product," *The Atlantic*, November 2009, pp. 36-38.

Meredith, Robyn, *The Elephant And The Dragon: The Rise Of India And China And What It Means To All Of Us*, New York: W.W.Norton and Company, 2007.

Millennium Development Goals: undp.org/mdg/basics.shtml

Millennium Goals Updates: mdgmonitor.org/index.cfm

More, Sir Thomas, *Utopia*, written in Latin, done into English by Ralph Robyson, Norwalk, CT: The Easton Press, 1963.

Mortenson, Greg, *Stones Into Schools*, New York: Viking Press, 2009.

Moyo, Dambisa, *Dead Aid: Why Aid Is Not Working And How There Is A Better Way For Africa*, New York: Farrar, Straus and Giroux, 2009.

Nachtwey, James and Alexander Fuller, "Mandela's Children," *National Geographic*, Vol 217, no. 6, June 2010, pp. 80-108.

Obama, Barak, *The Audacity Of Hope: Thoughts On Reclaiming The American Dream*, New York: Crown Publishers, 2006.

Pei, Minxin, *China's Trapped Transition: The Limits Of Developmental Autocracy*, Cambridge, MA: Harvard University Press, 2006.

Peleggi, Maurizio, *Thailand The Worldly Kingdom*, London: Reakton Books 2007.

Polak, Paul, *Out Of Poverty: What Works When Traditional Methods Fail*, San Francisco: Berrett-Koehler Publishers, Inc., 2008.

Reid, T.R., *The Healing Of America: A Global Quest For Better, Cheaper, And Fairer Health Care*, New York: The Penguin Press, 2009.

Russett, Bruce, Dean Acheson Professor of International Relations and Political Science, Yale University, Yale-Mount Holyoke Luncheon, Sarasota , FL, March 22, 2007.

Sachs, Jeffery, *The End Of Poverty*, New York: Penguin Books, 2006.

Sanger, David E. *The Inheritance: The World Obama Confronts And The Challenges To American Power*, New York: Harmony Books, 2009.

Schmemann, Serge, "Soul of Russia," *National Geographic*, Vol 215, no. 4, April 2009, pp. 112-137.

Seward, Jack, *The Japanese*, New York: William Morrow and Company, 1972.

Shelburne, Elizabeth Chiles, "The Next Breadbasket: How Africa Could Save the World—and Itself," *The Atlantic*, September 2009, pp. 72-73.

Smith, Adam, *An Inquiry Into The Nature And Causes Of The Wealth Of Nations*, New York: Random House, The Modern Library, 1994.

Sorman, Guy, "The Truth About China," *The Wall Street Journal*, Friday, April 22, 2007.

Statistical Yearbook: unstats.un.org/unsd/syb

Tata, Robert J., "Problems Of Industrial Old Age: New Britain, Ct, A Case Study," MA Thesis, Syracuse University, 1961.

———, *Haiti: Land Of Poverty*, Washington D.C.: University Press of America, 1982.

Tata, Robert J. and Ronald R. Schultz, "World Variation in Human Welfare: A New Index of Development Status," *Annals Of The Association Of American Geographers*, Vol 78, no. 4, December, 1988, pp. 580-593.

Teague, Matthew, "*The Other Tibet*," *National Geographic*, Vol 216, no. 6, December 2009, pp. 30-55.

Twain, Mark, *Autobiography*, edited by the Mark Twain Project at the Bancroft Library, Berkeley: University of California Press, 2010.

United Nations, *Charter Of The United Nations*, San Francisco: United Nations Conference on International Organization, 1945.

———, *United Nations Development Program, Human Development Report 2010*, Oxford: Oxford University Press 2010.

Universal Declaration of Human Rights: amnestyusa.org/print.php

Universal Islamic Declaration of Human Rights: mtpi.org

Veenhoven, Ruut, *World Database Of Happiness*, Erasmus University, Rotterdam, Holland.

Wallechinsky, David, "Is America Still No. 1," *Parade Magazine*, January 17, 2007, pp. 4-5.

Weiner, Eric, *The Geography Of Bliss: One Grump's Search For The Happiest Places In The World*, Thorndike, Maine: Center Point Publishing 2008.
Woodward, Bob, *Obama's Wars*, New York: Simon & Schuster, 2010.
World Bank Data: data.worldbank.org/indicator
World Database of Happiness: worlddatabaseofhappiness.eur.nl
Zakaria, Fareed, *The Post American World*, New York and London: W.H. Norton and Company, 2008

www.ingramcontent.com/pod-product-compliance
Ingram Content Group UK Ltd.
Pitfield, Milton Keynes, MK11 3LW, UK
UKHW012042150926
475560UK00001B/154

9 780761 859420